KOOTENAI BROWN

BY TONY HOLLIHAN

The Publisher: Folklore Publishing

National Library of Canada Cataloguing in Publication Data

Hollihan, K. Tony (Kelvin Tony), 1964–
  Kootenai Brown

  ISBN 1-894864-00-X

  1. Brown, John George, 1839–1916. 2. Frontier and pioneer life—Northwest, Canadian. 3. Frontier and pioneer life—West (U.S.) 4. Pioneers—Alberta—Biography. 5. Alberta—Biography. I. Title.
FC3672.1.B76H64 2001   971.23'02'092   C2002-910084-4
F1078.B76H64 2001

Photography Credits: Every effort has been made to accurately credit the sources of photographs. Any errors or omissions should be directed to the publisher for changes in future editions. *Photographs courtesy of* Glenbow Archives, Calgary, Canada (p. 10, NB-9-15; p. 36, NA-674-36; p. 42, NA-1798-14; p. 63, NA-2592-1; p. 70, NA-1315-28; p. 76, NA-325-9; p. 90, NA-659-15; p. 116, NA-1406-26; p. 139, NA-5501-13; p. 141, NA-2446-11; p. 162, NA-2631-1; p. 165, NA-619-2; p. 172, NA-619-3; p. 180, NA-1750-1; p. 197, NA-3321-8; p. 211, NA-250-103; p. 217, NA 2539-19; p. 229, NA-1687-43; p. 240, NA-1585-8; p. 245, NA-1253-3; p. 249, NA-2373-15); National Archives of Canada (p. 32, PA-61930; p. 29, C-44702; p. 124, C-47151; p. 158, PA-27161; p. 178, C-3031); Parks Canada Collection (p. 183); Provincial Archives of Alberta (p. 58, PA-6186); Provincial Archives of Manitoba (p. 129, N-461); Saskatchewan Archives Board (p. 122, R-A3955); Southern Pacific Photo, Union Pacific Historical Collection (p. 23, X-310); State Historical Society of North Dakota (p. 79, 78,121; p. 97, 1987.35.14); *The History of the Indian Mutiny* by Charles Ball, 1889 (p.15).

PC: P6

CONTENTS

FOREWORD

JOHN GEORGE BROWN, nicknamed in his later years and forever after remembered as Kootenai Brown, was born in 1839 in Ireland and died in the southern Alberta town of Fort Macleod in 1916. His itchy feet took him to India as an ensign in the British Army in the months following the Great Mutiny of the late 1850s and to Panama, San Francisco and Victoria as a roving adventurer in the early 1860s. He participated in the gold rushes in the interior of British Columbia as a miner, packer and police constable.

By the mid-1860s, Brown was hunting buffalo and fending off attacks from hostile Natives out on the plains. For a time he was a trader, exchanging whisky for furs with Native and Métis populations and immersing himself in the ways of his wife's people. He also worked for the U.S. Army as a mail carrier in Sioux country and survived a tense encounter with Sitting Bull. He learned to speak a number of Native languages to augment his Irish brogue.

A pivotal event in Brown's life was the murder of a trader in Montana in the mid-1870s. Brown stood trial and was acquitted, then fled back to Canada and settled in what was then known as the Kootenay Lakes region (see Author's Note, below). There he supported his family with hunting, trapping, fishing, guiding and trading. Brown's first wife was a Métis he called Olivia; they had two daughters and a son before Olivia died in 1885. He turned his children over to others to raise, apparently reasoning that it would be difficult for him to provide sufficient care and attention given his outdoors lifestyle. Later, he married a Cree whose English name was Isabella. Little more is known about Brown's family life.

Brown never turned away a drink or a race, preferring to pit his physical skills rather than his card-playing skills against those of a challenger. When the North-West Rebellion erupted in the spring of 1885, Brown joined up as a Rocky Mountain Ranger, patrolling the foothills and plains.

Brown was a colorful character, his scruffy moustache and slouchy hat almost becoming a trademark. He developed a reputation in southern Alberta as a font of local information. He became a warden and forestry and fishing officer, working hard to protect the pocket of the country he loved so much. His life encompassed the transition from the plains way of life to settlement, from hunting buffalo from the back of a horse to riding around in a car. He discarded the Anglicanism of his youth in favor of Theosophy, and he could spout Latin as fluently as he could cuss.

Kootenai Brown emerges as a legendary figure of the West. His enduring bequest has been the area he lobbied so strongly to protect, Waterton Lakes National Park, now a jewel in the crown of Rocky Mountain parks system.

AUTHOR'S NOTE ON PLACE NAMES: The name change from Kootenay Lakes to Waterton Lakes occurred near the end of Brown's life. For the sake of consistency, they will be referred to as the Kootenay Lakes throughout this book. As the reader will discover, Brown would have wanted it that way.

When Fort Macleod was incorporated as a town in 1892, "Fort" was unceremoniously dropped by locals who wanted to confine to the history books the wild, whoop-up image that they believed it suggested. Some years later, Macleod became a "Fort" once again. For the sake of continuity and clarity, "Fort Macleod" is used throughout this book.

JOHN GEORGE BROWN sat in the prisoner's dock. If he'd ever been in a lonelier place, he couldn't remember it. He chewed nervously on the drooping moustache that covered his lips. His eyes darted around the room, much in the fashion of an animal that'd just been caged. Images froze in his mind. A faded American flag and a framed picture of a man who Brown figured was the president of the United States were the only decorations on the wall. Below the flag sat the judge, a somber man in a black gown. His large wooden desk stood on carved lion paws and seemed to tower above the many onlookers who filled the court. Perched on the edge of the desk was the statue of a blindfolded woman holding the scales of justice. Brown hoped she could see his innocence through that blindfold. Off to Brown's right sat the 12-man jury. Brown refused to look into their eyes, afraid of what he might see there. And he was afraid of what they might see in his. He looked instead at the man being questioned on the witness stand.

"Mr. Healy, you are the sheriff of Fort Benton?" the prosecuting attorney asked.

"Yes, sir," Healy replied.

"We have already heard testimony as to the events of May 2, 1877. We know that the prisoner, John George Brown, brutally murdered Louis Ell. We know that the murder weapon was a knife. The prisoner has as much as admitted to the truth of these details. Can you tell us if your knowledge of Brown is consistent with these findings?"

"Brown is a vicious man," Healy replied, contempt thickening his voice. "As a sheriff, I've run into all sorts of characters. Many of 'em had souls blacker'n coal. But this Brown makes 'em all look like saints. He's a bad man and, as far as I can tell, he is without redeeming qualities. Louis Ell was a good man. Now, I'm not saying that Ell didn't have his problems. No man's perfect. But he deserved better than to be butchered by the likes of this animal."

"Thank you, Sheriff Healy. You may step down."

It's not true, Brown wanted to scream. *Ell asked for it!* Instead, he closed his eyes and found himself in a place he had once seen in his dreams. He stood above the Kootenay Lakes on the southeastern edge of Canada's Rocky Mountains. Brown had almost escaped to that place after he had killed Ell. The international boundary had been within his reach, and he had felt the breeze of freedom blowing from the north when he was captured.

"The jury has heard the evidence against John Brown," said the judge. "You may be excused for deliberation."

Brown was escorted back to his cell. The minutes passed like hours as he sat waiting for their verdict. He was alone; the jailer had explained to him that the practice was to place condemned men alone, especially when they had a history of self-abuse.

"Is the evidence against me really that persuasive?" asked Brown.

"I've seen men convicted on less," replied the jailer.

Brown's eyes followed an ant as it made its way to the center of the cell, picked up a crumb of food and left through a small crack on the base of the wall. *I'd give anything to change places with that ant*, Brown thought.

The clanging of the jailer's key brought Brown back to reality. "It's time, Brown."

Within a few moments, Brown was again seated in the prisoner's dock.

"Will the prisoner please rise," commanded the judge. "Gentlemen of the jury, have you reached a verdict?"

"We have, your honor," the jury foreman replied.

"Is it unanimous?"

"It is, your honor."

"Please read it."

As the foreman unfolded the small piece of paper, Brown's knees turned to jelly and he reached to the rail before him for support. His eyes focused on the small patch of blue sky just visible through the courtroom's only window. His chest was frozen still.

LIFE BEFORE BRITISH NORTH AMERICA
1839–62

BROWN WAS DRINKING in the saloon of the Macleod Hotel, and that was hardly surprising. If he was in town and his work was done, Brown could pretty much always be found there. Hell...even if his work wasn't done, the likelihood of finding him there was pretty damn good. And if someone else was buying the whisky, odds were good that Brown obliged with a story.

"So it's my Indian adventures you're interested in?" Brown asked the young man who had been so generous about buying his drinks. He took off the Stetson he donned whenever he was in town. Dragging his hand through his long, dark hair, Brown said, "Stories are best told under the sun or moon, where there's ample space for them to spread out. Let's go for a stroll, and I'll tell you about my time in India."

Drinks in hand, the two men headed out into the welcoming night. "You probably know that I ended up in India as a member of Her Majesty's finest. But I'll wager you don't know that the army was never my first choice. It was

Fort Macleod, Alberta, is located on the Oldman River, 165 kilometers (100 miles) south of Calgary. Law and order are embedded in the city's foundations. The original fort was founded by Assistant Commissioner James F. Macleod, the commanding officer of the first North-West Mounted Police contingent to settle in the region. Built by the Mounties in 1874, it was the first police post in present-day Alberta and served as the force's national headquarters from 1876 to 1878. One major problem with the fort in its early years was that its location on an island in the Oldman River made it susceptible to flooding during the river's annual spring swelling. A decade later, the Mounties finally moved the fort to its present location. By then, early settlement around the fort had begun to evolve into an independent community. In 1892 Fort Macleod was incorporated as a town, and five years later its future was secured when the Canadian Pacific Railway built a station there. By the turn of the century, Fort Macleod was well on its way to becoming a service center for the farms and ranches in the region.

more of a shotgun weddin'. It's not original to say that circumstances have a funny way of directing choices, but it's
true nonetheless."

Brown took another long swig of his whisky as a far-
away, dreamy look came into his eyes. "For me," he continued, "those circumstances included a sweet young thing
from Liscannor, just across the bay from my own dear
Ennistymon. I remember as if it were yesterday, the two of
us perched atop the Cliffs of Moher, our whispers fallin' to
the ocean's spray far below. Ah, we were young. And we
were discreet, but the fruit, shall I say, of our love was all too
evident," said a winking Brown. "I'm not proud of it, and I
still get a little red in the face when I think about it, but a
life with a raggedy brood, spent mucking in the ground for
smelly potatoes, was not for me. So I made my escape with
the army.

"Before I knew it, we were shipped to the mysterious
east. We made our way south, and after some weeks finally
swung east around the African horn. Many of the boys lost
hope near the Cape of Good Hope, but not me. I grew
fond of the quiet nights above deck, of the stars that lit our
way. I still feel that there are few things that can stir the soul
like a clear, starry night. It gives a man a powerful connection with forces greater than us," Brown murmured, his
eyes focused on some long-ago memory.

"India was a place of dreams," he said in a low voice,
swatting at a mosquito on his neck. "By the time I arrived,
the Great Mutiny was already over and our duties were
mostly those of policing. The defeated Indians proved a
docile group, so we spent most of our time pursuing more
amiable recreations. We relaxed under large fans that made a
gentle breeze through the tireless efforts of an unseen
punkah wallah. We listened lazily to the high pitch of sitars
and sucked on bubbling hookahs. When the mood took us,

we hunted great white-striped tigers with our dogs. As we rode, cheroots dangled from our lips, the pungent tobacco taking our minds off the heat of the day. Men in turbans rode high on bellowing elephants or sat nestled on lanky camels. Beautiful women wore intricate designs tattooed on their skin. It was a mystical place, one that has affected my own spirituality deeply," said Brown, a serious tone infusing his words.

For a few moments, Brown chewed absently on the ends of his moustache and seemed as if he had lost the thread of his story somewhere in the distant past. "I might've happily stayed there forever," he said at last, "but that was not to be. A fellow officer, I forget his name, besmirched my honor. You see, I had been given an elephant by a rajah. An elephant, yes! The animal was a gift for helping his son out of a jam. Let me tell you, you haven't ridden until you've sat high on the neck of an elephant. The beasts only lumber along, but you're on top of the world." As he spoke, Brown bounced along as if he were once again high atop the great gray beast.

"Anyway, this officer suggested that I had come by the beast in a dishonest fashion, and he was none too timid about spreading nasty rumors to that effect. That was something I simply was not going to stand for," Brown scowled. "He wouldn't eat his words, so he ate my lead," he told his spellbound audience.

"Having chosen such a course of action, I knew that there was nothing left for me but flight. With the aid of a young mercenary soldier, I disguised myself as a local and headed for Calcutta. Once there I made quick arrangements to leave on a southbound windjammer that was laden with a cargo of nitrates. Its departure came none too soon. As we made our way out the narrows, I looked back and saw the better part of a small British detachment swarm onto the wharf. They jumped and shouted and waved their arms wildly, but I broke into a salty song to keep the crew's attention." Here Brown interrupted his tale to belt out a few scratchy bars of the ribald tune, then threw his head back and howled with laughter. "Good thing I did, too—otherwise, the crew might've let loose with a round or two of ammo, and the skirmish would've surely sent up the whole harbor!"

More serious, he continued, "The windjammer was a fine, sleek vessel and we soon made port in Madras. The streets that fed that harbor town brought all sorts of flotsam and jetsam to the shore. It wasn't a place where one walked at night, and I tried to stay put even during the day. Even then I hardly felt safe. But I had to find a way out of the country, so I sought out a seagoing vessel. I was lucky enough to sign on with a sloop headed for South America. After a month of easy sailing, we ran up against foul weather off the Falkland Islands and were shipwrecked on a tiny piece of dry land that wasn't much more than a mud stain on the Atlantic."

Brown paused. "The throat's a bit dry. How about we take detour back to the saloon? You'll be buying?"

ᔕᔕ

A few of the details in Brown's story were real enough, but the truth about the man is found in the storytelling itself. Brown loved to spin a yarn and, as he aged, both fact and fiction figured prominently in what he claimed were his experiences. Blarney was his constant companion. And even if he was inclined to keep matters on the straight and narrow, others repeating his stories often weren't. As Brown's legend grew, folks who spoke of him tended to add their own embellishments to his biography as if they were the authors of Brown's life story. In the case of his military posting in India, the reality was somewhat less colorful than the stories many people came to accept as true.

Brown joined Number 12 Company of the First Battalion Eighth Regiment in January 1858. The enlistment was another link in a chain of family military service; his grandfather and uncle had decades of army experience in lands as diverse as South Africa, the West Indies and the Canadas. Still, the road to military employment was not an easy one. Brown's parents had died when he was young, perhaps victims of the Irish potato famine or the disease that swept along in its wake. He was raised by his maternal grandmother, Bridget Sophia Finucane, at Munroe House in Ennistymon, County Clare, along the western coast of Ireland. Only Bridget's dogged determination garnered Brown a military posting; contrary to legend, it had nothing to do with a romantic encounter gone wrong. Once Brown turned 16, Bridget initiated her efforts to obtain a commission for him. A necessary first step was to take the required exams at Royal Military College at Sandhurst. Brown did so and passed with the greatest possible credit. However, a commission was not readily forthcoming without money. It had to be purchased, and Brown's family was not blessed with great fortune. As a result, Bridget Sophia became his tireless advocate. Between November 1855 and December 1857, she deluged military officials with a series of letters, highlighting her family's military service and berating the army's cold, unsympathetic attitude. In her mind, it was only proper that young John be given an opportunity. While her missives might well have been influential, it was the Great Indian Mutiny that prompted the army to change its mind. Badly in need of soldiers, the army commissioned Brown as an ensign without purchase on December 13, 1857.

The Great Indian Mutiny was unique because of popular support it received from both Indian civilians and military. In the 1840s and 1850s, the ruling British introduced changes that upset many Indians. They abolished local traditions such as *suttee* (the Hindu practice of a widow sacrificing herself on her husband's funeral pyre) and *thagi* (ritual murder and robbery by gangs in central India in the name of Kali, the Hindu goddess of destruction). As well, the army ordered Sepoys—Indian mercenary soldiers, who were the backbone of the British military—to serve for extended periods with limited pay in territories that were not their homelands. These unwelcome directives caused resignations en masse. Matters worsened when the military introduced the Enfield rifle. Soldiers had to bite off the end of the rifle's cartridge to expose the powder, and they believed that the cartridges were greased with the fat of pigs and cows. The former was unclean to Muslims and the latter holy to Hindus. Many Sepoys, who refused to touch the Enfield cartridges, were imprisoned and court-martialled. Sympathetic Sepoys broke them out and the bloodshed began.

Brown spent the first months of 1858 at Chatham, in southeastern coastal England, learning the basics of soldiering and leading troops. In September, his company finally received its sailing orders, and the men made their way from Gravesend to Calcutta. When the troops set out aboard the *Octavio*, Brown was put in charge of a 21-man unit for the duration of the voyage. The men were happy to be freed from their training exercises and anxious to join their brethren in the First Battalion, who were busy quelling the Indian Mutiny.

The spring and summer of 1858 were bleak seasons for the British Empire. The Sepoys outnumbered its forces at a ratio of about eight to one; in the northeast regions where the fighting was most intense, British odds were even less favorable. Whole garrisons were wiped out. The families of British soldiers and any other Christians unfortunate enough to be found were killed. Indian princes fanned the flames of the mutiny in an effort to regain the authority they had lost to the British. The British used every tactic at their disposal to reassert their own authority. A popular deterrent was to tie the mutineers to cannons and blow them to bits. The effectiveness of the messy punishment lay in the Sepoys' belief that a spiritual destruction accompanied such a physical one; a body destroyed meant a spirit without a future. By the fall of 1858, the British had finally brought the rebels under control.

After a long journey—the only break likely coming from a brief provisioning call at Simon's Bay, an East India Company port on the southwest coast of Africa near the Cape of Good Hope—Brown and his company arrived at Calcutta in February 1859. They were greeted with the news of the Sepoys' defeat. This turn of events was surely disappointing. Many a boring day aboard the *Octavio* must have been spent planning military strategies or playing out imagined battlefield scenarios. With the mutiny over, the excitement that had coursed through the soldiers' veins dissipated. They found themselves operating as an army under peacetime conditions, policing a people for whom the wounds of defeat were still raw.

The recent arrivals marched to Fattehguhr, in north-central India southeast of Lucknow, where they joined the main part of the regiment on February 3. For Brown and his compatriots, the irritation of bowel discomfort and the tremors of fever replaced the excitement of battle. The closest thing to physical action was seen in the local brothel, and many a soldier soon bore wounds of the venereal kind. Long hours were spent observing local people and their customs, writing letters home or hunting. Brown was drawn to eastern mysticism. It was an interest that was to later flower in his adoption of Theosophy, a religion with significant parallels to the spiritualism he discovered in India.

The Eighth Regiment was called home in December 1859 with all the pomp and ceremony of pageantry that only the Victorian British could muster. Lord Clyde, commander of the British forces in India, inspected the regiment. Such an occasion was rare, and it was undoubtedly designed to pay official recognition to the regiment's 14 years of service. Lady Canning, wife of the governor general of India, later threw a farewell ball where eating delicacies and dancing with refined young women must surely have provided a welcome change to the soldiers' otherwise dull life of orders and routine.

The first of the regiment reached Calcutta in February 1860. While they awaited transport, a call went out for volunteers to fight in the Second Chinese War. Brown declined the offer. Perhaps he had already concluded that military life was not for him. On April 5, Brown and the last of the regiment boarded the *Clara* and made for England. The journey was punctuated by a call to the island of St. Helena in the South Atlantic. The soldiers marched from Jamestown to the Valley of the Geraniums, where Napoleon had once been interred (he died there in 1821 but was reburied in France in 1840). After the men paid their respects, the journey continued and the *Clara* finally reached home in September.

ᗡᗡ

Without the excitement of imminent warfare that had accompanied the easterly voyage, the four-month voyage from Calcutta to Spithead in England must have been tedious. At best it provided plenty of opportunity for a thoughtful man to consider his future. Brown's actions after arriving in Gosport, where his troop was stationed for the next eight months, suggest that he decided while on the journey or almost immediately thereafter to leave the army. The purchase system of advancement still dictated promotion in the British forces, and for a low-ranking officer with a limited income there was simply no future in the service. The cost of graduating from an ensigncy to a lieutenancy was in the neighborhood of £300, a king's ransom to a man like Brown. It was a sum that he would never accumulate on his meager pay. It's also likely that Brown found the regimentation and close quarters of military life unappealing; while he never discussed such feelings, the solitary and remote life he subsequently chose to lead certainly hints at them. As for the adventure…well, one didn't have to be in the army to see the world. The second half of the 19th century was ripe with opportunity for those who were willing to take a chance.

Brown's greatest challenge came not in taking chances or seizing opportunities but in severing the ties that bound him to military service. Surely he had great difficulty telling his grandmother that he was leaving the army. Brown was well aware of the considerable effort Bridget Sophia had exerted to get him into the army, so breaking the news of his decision to her could not have been easy. That challenge probably explains the three leaves that Brown took in quick succession. He spent Christmas of 1860 back at Munroe House, and he was there again in March and September 1861. One suspects that the frequent visits were not merely designed to tell his grandmother the stories of his Indian expedition. Rather, he was likely sharing his disconcerting news. After transferring to Templemore in Ireland, Brown finally resigned in September 1861. Bridget Sophia died at the end of January 1862. By then Brown had departed for the far-off gold fields in British Columbia, never to return to the Emerald Isle.

Brown made his way west with Arthur Vowell, with whom he shared a history. Vowell was Irish and had served in the military, both in India and in Ireland. The two were likely acquainted long before their departure. They made their way to the Panama Isthmus, a three-week journey from Ireland on a ship of either the Royal Mail Steam Packet Company or the Panama Railway. The sighting of the New World must have been a thrilling experience, but the lush, green, Eden-like landscape that rose from the clear blue Caribbean Sea gave little indication as to the true nature of the land and its people.

The men disembarked at Colon, on the east side of the isthmus. Their plan was to ride the Panama Railroad from there to Culebra, the western terminus located just beyond Panama City. From there they would continue north to British North America. American interests had laid the

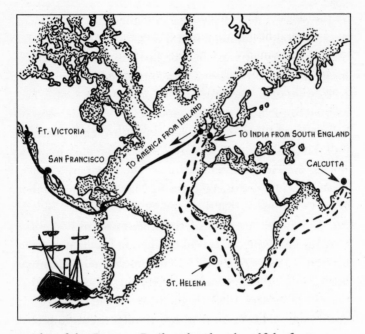

tracks of the Panama Railroad only a handful of years earlier, having foreseen profit in the short land route to the Pacific Ocean. Rumor had it that a man died for every railway tie laid, most of them victims of disease-carrying mosquitoes. Brown had little trouble with the winged carriers of death because his short stay occurred during the rainy season.

Upon landing, the men discovered that their departure would be delayed, so they did a little exploring. Renting a narrow canoe, they made their way up the Charges River, which gave easy access well into the interior of the isthmus. They continued on past Fort San Lorenzo, which stood an eerie and lonely sentry atop a steep overlooking hill. It was a reminder of the old Spanish empire, a small wooden castle built during Phillip II's reign to protect the mouth of the river from pirates. Along the way, they hunted with their ball and cap rifles and brought down some deer, wild turkey and even an alligator. They discovered something of the singularity of tropical heat as they poled along; it was oppressively hot, and the humidity weighed heavily on the men.

"It looks like we're going to get some rain, Arthur," said Brown, looking heavenward. "It's getting black and the sky'll surely open."

A crack of thunder split open the dark clouds and rain started to fall in sheets. The men held their faces high in anticipation of the watery relief.

"Shite! The bloody rain is scalding! Let's get out of this mess," exclaimed Brown as he pulled his slouch hat down over his forehead. They headed for the shelter of elm trees along the river's bank.

Having had enough adventure for the time being, Brown and Vowell returned to Colon and boarded the railway. The engines burned wood, so it was slow going; one 25-mile (40 km) stretch took no less than four hours to complete. Daylight regularly disappeared as the train made its way through dense jungle. Upon reaching Panama, they found a respectable enough station. At two storeys, it stood above the surrounding dwellings but was still small enough to enjoy the shelter of an imposing palm tree. White businessmen operated the few stores. Walking around town, Brown and Vowell saw barefoot soldiers dressed in khaki and locals engaged in the popular recreation of cock fighting. Women strolled with baskets of fruit and other goods balanced on their heads. Clothing was tattered and smiles were few. To Brown's eyes, these were some of the most miserable people he ever had the misfortune to see—and Brown had seen the devastating effects of the potato famine in Ireland.

The rail journey was costly—it took $25 out of each man's pocket. Still, it was less than the amount they had to fork over to the Pacific Mail Steamship Company to get to

San Francisco on the next leg of the journey. When they finally reached Culebra, some 65 kilometers of track behind them, they discovered that the cheapest ticket to the northern port was $52. They bit their tongues, grudgingly paid the fee, boarded a steamer and bid farewell to Panama.

Brown and Vowell landed in San Francisco just as the city was completing its metamorphosis from an urban hodgepodge to a regional economic force. In the mid-1840s, the local population numbered less than 500. Just 20 years later, some 40,000 called the city home. The impetus for this explosion was the discovery of gold at Sutter's Mill in 1848. A few days after the discovery, Mexico ceded the territory to the United States, setting the scene for rapid immigration. Those suffering from gold fever came in the thousands from China, Australia, Europe and the Americas. In 1849 alone, estimates suggest that nearly 45,000 found their way to Frisco. They still had to make their way inland to the gold fields of the rivers and mountains to the east, but their initial presence in the coastal city proved transformational.

San Francisco was a violent place, and blood was shed from the waterfront up to the ethnic enclaves of tent shantytowns, north to Telegraph Hill and south of Market Street. Miners were not known for their civility, and those who made their living off the workers were no less explosive. The establishment of law and order failed to match the arrival of the miners, and vandalism, theft, rape and murder were part and parcel of life in the boomtown. Bloodletting extended beyond the rough and ready folks who gave the city its boom origins and into the classes of the refined. A few years before Brown's arrival, a member of the state Supreme Court gunned down the political "boss" of Frisco in a duel; the prize was control of the local Democratic Party.

The panorama of San Francisco's waterfront was certainly not characterized by anything resembling urban planning. The shoreline was extended into the harbor as new wharves were built and the shallow Yerba Buena Cove was filled. Because vessels were required to anchor a good distance from shore, piers of different lengths and widths soon reached out into the harbor to give disembarking passengers easier access. Of course, these wooden entryways were privately owned, long since staked as personal property by speculators who were always alert to the smell of money. Many sought to avoid the price gouging and chose to live on their vessels. The result was a ramshackle waterfront, a jungle of saloons, grocery stores, commission houses, brothels and disorderly seaside establishments designed mostly to make a quick buck. As land became unavailable to prospective entrepreneurs, boats of various sizes were brought close to shore, scuttled and permanently anchored to serve as businesses similar to those on shore.

When Brown arrived in 1862, the forty-niners were already a memory. Gold seekers had turned east to Colorado and Nevada and north to British Columbia; San Francisco was transforming into a metropolitan center whose economy depended upon agriculture, manufacturing and transportation. Brown and Vowell had no interest in San Francisco per se, and their visit to the port was merely a hiccup in their grander plans. They simply needed to build up a stake that would allow them to continue north to the gold fields of British Columbia. It was therefore imperative that they find jobs. Fortunately, work was plentiful; before long, both men were employed as skinners, driving a horse team that hauled furs and skins from the old wharf up to the city's business district. It was difficult and unpleasant work, especially because the two were green when it came to operating a horse team. Their initiation into horsemanship was nothing if not challenging. The old wharf was a collection of jutting piles, sharp angles and rotting timber planks, so it took considerable skill to maneuver a team while ensuring that none of the horses would trip or plunge through a hole and break a leg. Only the liberal use of profanities and a judicious application of the whip brought any success.

This working environment brought Brown and Vowell into regular contact with the worst that the city had to offer. The area that extended from the old wharf to the lower part of the city was the location of San Francisco's gold-mining beginnings, and it continued to house the tough and the transient. Rare was the day when one didn't discover that a companion had mysteriously disappeared overnight, a victim of the harbor front's routine malice. While Brown and Vowell were undoubtedly attracted to the gaming establishments, saloons and houses of ill-repute that proliferated, they somehow managed to keep their roving eyes fixed on the goal of building up a stake. It was only a matter of weeks before the pair had saved enough money to continue their journey. They didn't have enough to make a go of gold mining, but their funds were sufficient to allow them to abandon Frisco's smelly bowels and to complete their journey to British Columbia. In mid-February, they each paid their $25 for steerage tickets and boarded the *Brother Jonathan*, bound once again for Queen's country and the comfortable environs of empire.

The Gold Rush
1862-64

"GOLD!" trumpeted the news accounts. "Gold! British Columbia's Fraser River to be the next El Dorado! Discoveries of the mineral already dwarf California findings!" As reports raged across the world, men of all ages were drawn to the Fraser and later to the Cariboo, in the mainland interior of the Pacific colony. Whether they were looking to make a quick buck, or they were down and out, or they were simply seeking adventure, the news made grown men giddy and smart men silly. Any obstacle—be it distance, cost or hard work—faded in the bright and blinding rays cast by the yellow ore. When people were infected with gold fever, their only remedy was to build up a stake and make a claim. John Brown was just one of the great number of miners who did exactly that and changed the course of the region's history.

At the time of the gold rush, the European presence along what is known today as coastal British Columbia was a relatively recent phenomenon. While there were rumors that Russian *promyshlenniki* (fur hunters and traders) were active in the region in the late 17th century, it wasn't until the late 18th century that non-Natives officially began to trade there. In addition to the Russians, the most active were the Americans and the British. Each group was represented by large fur-trading interests: the Russian-American Company (Russia), the American Fur Company (United States) and the Hudson's Bay Company (England). The region held great economic possibility because fur resources were abundant. Especially promising was the sea otter trade; this coastal mammal was found in seemingly limitless numbers, and its pelt was much coveted in the vast Asian marketplace. Perhaps more importantly, the local Native peoples were anxious and willing to trade.

By the late 1830s, successful negotiations between the Hudson's Bay Company and the Russian-American Company ensured that Russian trade was limited to north of the top of Vancouver Island. British and American concerns clashed for control of the remainder of the lucrative trade. The HBC sought to consolidate its position by establishing trading posts in the Oregon Territory, which was at that time north of American activities. As a result, the British controlled the coastal trade in the Pacific Northwest for the first decades of the 19th century. However, U.S. interest in the region was strong and Americans were soon active there. The British presence failed to douse Yankee enthusiasm. Matters came to a head in the mid-1840s, when James Polk was elected president of the United States on a policy of geographic expansion. Polk wanted to annex all land below the southerly reaches of Russian control, but he became preoccupied with American efforts in Mexico. Ultimately, he settled for a mutually agreeable northern boundary following the 49th parallel, as set out in the 1846 Treaty of Oregon. Aware that the loss of the Oregon Territory was inevitable, the HBC in the early 1840s

moved its main headquarters from Fort Vancouver, near the
mouth of the Columbia River, to Fort Victoria, on the
southern tip of Vancouver Island. The relocation was followed by an agreement between the Hudson's Bay
Company and the British government, which gave the
trading company control over the entire island. Within a
decade, Fort Victoria was solidly established as the center
for the Hudson's Bay Company operations in the Pacific.

A significant clause in the agreement between the
Hudson's Bay Company and the imperial government
required that the company actively solicit settlers. The HBC
was not keen on this clause because settlers inevitably
meant farming, laws and government. Any such developments were, in the company's considered economic opinion, a threat to the company's bottom line. George
Simpson, the "Little Dictator" who was governor of the
HBC from 1821 to 1860, privately indicated that no real
effort was to be made to encourage immigration. The businessman in Simpson knew that even if the HBC's rights in
the region were eventually terminated for non-fulfillment
of its obligations, the intervening years would likely see the
area trapped out and of little value. Instead, the HBC
turned to its employees and encouraged retired company
men to settle in the area. Such folks were a known quantity,
and it was anticipated that the policy would lead to minimal disruption of HBC activities.

Settlement soon spilled outside the confines of Fort
Victoria's walls. British men all, the settlers' backgrounds
cut across the divides of social and economic position. As a
result, British metropolitan influences wove their way
through the fabric of the small but growing community.
Schools, churches and local government were established
and the town slowly transformed into something akin to
what one might stumble upon in the English heartland.

Sir George Simpson (1787–1860), governor of the Hudson's Bay Company in British North America, was among the most powerful men in the colonies. But he did not attain that position in the conventional way. Simpson had never been a trader unlike most appointees to higher positions in the HBC. He was an administrator, effective and ruthless. He arrived in Rupert's Land in 1820 at the high point of the struggle between the HBC and the North West Company for control of the fur trade. In 1821, when the HBC emerged victorious, Simpson was made governor of the Northern Department. He was charged with introducing measures that would increase profits. He was so effective that five years later he was given command of HBC operations in North America, a position he held until his death in 1860. Simpson traveled widely through HBC holdings, but never with his wife, for fear that she might discover his numerous infidelities with Native women.

THE VICTORIA SENTINEL

GOLD DISCOVERED ON FRASER RIVER

Shiploads of prospectors arriving daily at Fort Victoria. Thousands expected to buoy local economy.

James Douglas, the chief factor of Fort Victoria facilitated the process of settlement with his efforts and foresight. Douglas, whom Brown referred to as the "head bamboo chief," recognized Native sovereignty in the region and set about signing treaties to make sure that land was available for settlers to buy. Thus, the transition from frontier to civilization began smoothly.

The community's steady and sure development was interrupted, and ultimately transformed, with the reports of gold. Fort Victoria became the gateway to the gold fields on the mainland, a role secured by a directive from the colonial government that made it illegal to transport goods into the region except by way of the island port. In the mid-1850s, the non-Native population numbered about 200; by decade's end, with the Fraser River gold rush in full steam, there were thousands. The variety of nationalities gave a cosmopolitan appearance to the once-uniformly British community, and Brits soon found themselves working shoulder to shoulder with Germans, Italians, Chinese, Spaniards and Americans—representatives from all reaches of the globe. Many of the original British settlers were uncomfortable with these strange newcomers and fearful that "foreigners" might precipitate undesirable changes. James Douglas, who by this time had resigned from his position in the Hudson's Bay Company to serve as governor of the coastal colonies, took quick and forceful action. His directives ensured that the imprint of Britishness, if not the smell of roast beef itself, would be found from rolling Pacific to rugged mountaintop. It is not difficult to imagine Douglas, who was rarely accused of restraint, asserting his wishes in a booming voice.

"We will suffer neither the lawlessness of the California frontier nor the embarrassment of the Oregon Territory. This is British soil and, by God, the rule of law will be applied. It will be found alive on the banks of every gurgling stream, on the pitted walls of every dark tunnel, within the confines of every gambling establishment and grog house. Not a person will not know that he is in the Queen's country!"

Douglas wanted to ensure that the law would have a visible physical presence. To that end, Matthew Baillie Begbie, educated at Cambridge and a recent London barrister, accepted Her Majesty's appointment as judge of British Columbia. The performance of his duties would require him to ride the circuit, in the grand tradition of the English justices. It was envisioned that his regular presence would make certain that those miners, and any others, unfamiliar with the ways of acceptable British citizenship would quickly learn the boundaries of proper behavior. But Judge Begbie was only one man, and his efforts were to be complemented by those of a corps of gold commissioners who

Sir James Douglas (1803–1877) was the most powerful man in the British territory of the Pacific Northwest. In 1839, he was appointed HBC's chief factor at Fort Vancouver on the Columbia River. Later he oversaw the transfer of HBC operations to Vancouver Island, continuing on as supervisor of the fur trade from Fort Victoria. In 1851 the Queen appointed Douglas as the colony's governor and seven years later he was sworn in as governor of the new mainland colony of British Columbia, at which point he had to sever his ties with the HBC. During Douglas' tenure, his greatest challenges were the series of gold rushes that exploded in the late 1850s, especially the Fraser River and the Cariboo. His guiding principle was that the gold rush not undermine British authority on the mainland. To that end he created effective judicial and transportation systems. Douglas retired in 1863, amidst pressures for a less autocratic government and charges of spending irregularities. He is considered by many to be the father of British Columbia.

were responsible for ensuring that the extraction of gold was done in an orderly, civilized fashion. Finally, constables were assigned to actively maintain the peace throughout the land.

The governor might well have bellowed, "Let no man doubt that although the flowers of the British countryside bloom thousands of miles away, should that man close his eyes and inhale deeply, it will be as if he is standing knee deep in the fragrant heather!"

The influx of miners, combined with the order imposed by Douglas, provided a climate that encouraged new growth. Fort Victoria was joined by a tent town that blossomed overnight. Construction boomed, and the number of buildings grew from dozens to hundreds. Commerce flourished as experienced entrepreneurs set up shop. Miners had to have their supplies, and many of the fortunes made during the gold rush were those of men who never set foot in the gold fields. The lifeblood of the boom, however, was the miner himself. Some of the more experienced miners—those who had "seen the elephant," it was said—brought with them the supplies that they knew were necessary to properly exploit their claims. Others had money and were able to purchase what was needed. For both these groups, Fort Victoria served as little more than a brief but necessary stop on their way to the mainland. For many others, the destitute who came with just the clothes on their backs and the dreams in their hearts, the town became a temporary home. There they sought work to earn the money required to travel up the Fraser River and into the Cariboo. The steadfast remained true to their goal, while others fell victim to the variety of temptations and treacheries that infested boomtowns. More than one would-be miner found his dreams delayed, or terminated, before he had a chance to swing a pick, slide a sluice gate or shake a pan.

ᔓᔔ

In February 1862, the steamer *Brother Jonathan*, one of
the numerous ships that offered regular passage to miners
departing to the north from San Francisco, arrived in
Victoria. Among its many passengers seeking fortune and
adventure were John Brown and his traveling companion
Arthur Vowell. They arrived as the Cariboo gold rush was
about to crest; in 1863 nearly $4 million worth of the ore
would be mined. In subsequent years, discoveries tapered
off, and by the mid-1860s, the rush was played out. But in
the heady years of the early 1860s, the glitter of gold still
sparkled in men's eyes and there was a definite sense that
dreams could turn into realities.

Shipping goods from Victoria to the farthest reaches of
mining up the Fraser River cost 10 times as much as shipping the same goods from London to Victoria. Once the
goods landed in the mining communities, the laws of supply and demand operated, and rarely was the former found
to be any match for the latter. Unscrupulous upriver businessmen also did their best to manipulate costs, and rare was
the miner who avoided, for example, paying extra money
for tobacco that was soaked in the river overnight so that it
might weigh more at the time of sale. Combined, these factors resulted in inland prices for goods that bore little
resemblance to coastal charges.

The journey to Victoria had all but exhausted Brown's
and Vowell's savings, so they found it necessary to remain in
town for several months to work at building up a new
stake. Mining was an expensive undertaking, and Brown
was starting from scratch, having arrived dressed in rags
with only 50¢ and a good pair of boots to his name. He'd
need much more than that. Green as they might be to this
line of work, Brown and Vowell were aware that only the

foolhardy ventured inland without sufficient funds. However, in the boom-time economy of the rush, impediments to finding work were few and insignificant to the determined, and the necessary stake could be accumulated rapidly by those willing to put their backs into it. Brown spent the spring chopping poles—the backbone of the tent town— and successfully resisted the many earthier temptations that might interfere with his gold-mining aspirations. By the summer of 1862, he and Vowell had begun their journey up the Fraser River.

The men soon discovered that, in the Cariboo, living was expensive but life was cheap. Stories of murder and theft floated down the Fraser as regularly as the driftwood caught in its current. And to Brown's and Vowell's chagrin, the opportunities for mining were not as plentiful as they had expected. Most of the riverside far up the Fraser had been long since staked out by others chasing similar dreams. Neither man had a fat bankroll to buy out an accessible claim. The challenge proved too great for Vowell and he soon returned to Victoria, finding employment with the burgeoning civil service. Brown, however, was born under a wandering star, and his roving disposition prevented him from making a similar retreat. He continued on up the Fraser until he was able to hook up with a transportation company that freighted goods up the mighty river.

There were many such operations on the Fraser because river transport was the only way communities and miners upstream could get supplies. It wasn't easy work, though, and despite the good money, only a man broke and down on his luck would be desperate enough to take the job. Brown fit this description, so he signed on with an outfit that ran the 40 kilometers between Kanaka Bar and Boston Bar. Hauling the freight was physically demanding work. The gear was packed on canoes carved from the huge cedars

Running 650 kilometers along the Fraser River Canyon between Yale and Barkerville, the Cariboo Road was built as a wagon route to the gold fields of the Cariboo region. The road was conceived by Governor James Douglas, who believed that a well-constructed transportation route into British Columbia's interior would increase his authority over the region and ensure that the colony remained under British control. The road also made the Cariboo more accessible to miners, reducing their transportation costs, and thus making them less likely to cause trouble. In 1862 the Royal Engineers surveyed the road and completed work on the route's two most difficult stretches: the 10 kilometers from Yale to Boston Bar and the 15 kilometers from Cook's Ferry along the Thompson River. The remainder of the road was completed by private contractors in 1865. Because the proposed route was often along precipices or blocked by solid rock that had to be blasted, it was an expensive undertaking at more than $1.25 million.

that grew in the area. Brown's vessel was nine meters long, with a two-meter beam. Though the cedar craft were much more cumbersome than the birchbark canoes used by the Natives to the east (canoes that could carry about the same amount of freight) only the cedar vessels could withstand the merciless pounding of the Fraser. Sturdiness was a real concern because the stretch of river between Kanaka Bar and Boston Bar was all white water, a matter of geography that added its own problems. Brown knew the risks firsthand. A particularly challenging part of the downstream river was called Hell's Gate, a name perfectly descriptive of the terrifying and unwelcome rapids. Brown once stood by helplessly as he and some co-workers watched a canoe overturn and the 13-man crew drown.

"That current's so strong, I expect those bodies will be washed out into the Gulf of George," Brown reflected to a nearby companion. Silently he gave thanks that his route was well to the north.

To fight through the powerful downstream currents, the canoe was cord-led upriver, a method of transportation that required part of the crew to work onshore and haul the vessel to its destination with long ropes. When the crew encountered the many sections of the river too shallow or turbulent for the vessel to easily pass, the canoe had to be unloaded. The men were forced to pack the freight the necessary distance, often almost two kilometers, in the tradition of the voyageurs of old. Each crewmember had to lug up to about 70 kilograms of gear over often mountainous terrain that even a horse would shy away from. The current was such that it took some four and a half days to reach the upriver destination, but the return journey was made in two and a half hours!

Brown made $6 a day (a good salary) pushing freight, but with winter came the shutdown in mining operations

STORE

BARKERVILLE

N

QUESNEL

SWIFT RIVER

GOLD

QUESNEL RIVER

WILLIAMS LAKE

MENEFEE'S
MISSION CREEK
HOUSE

CHILCOTIN RIVER

100 MILE HOUSE

CARIBOO ROAD

FRASER RIVER

LILLOOET

THOMPSON RIVER

FT. KAMLOOPS

LYTTON

KANAKA BAR

BOSTON BAR

HELL'S GATE CANYON

FT. VANCOUVER

YALE

HOPE

CANADA

FT. LANGLEY

U.S.A.

FT. VICTORIA

FT. VICTORIA

and little demand for goods upriver. He again found himself out of a job. Searching for work, he made his way into and then around the Cariboo. Travel in the region was much less difficult since the discovery of gold. Under the direction of Governor Douglas, who believed that effective control of the gold fields required adequate transportation routes, an excellent system of trails had been established and criss-crossed the region. The main routes were the responsibility of the British government's Royal Engineers, but often trails were built with the great encouragement of the local entrepreneurs whose roadhouses peppered the region. These establishments varied in size and respectability, but for the most part they were simple gathering places for lonely miners seeking entertainment, companionship, food, supplies or the rare luxury of something solid over their heads and soft under their backs for the night.

In the late fall of 1862, Brown found himself at Menefee's Mission Creek Roadhouse, just east of the Fraser River near Williams Lake. Like so many of the roadhouses, Menefee's was strategically located at the junction of two well-traveled trails, in this case the Brigade and the Davidson. A site on the trails was key to the economic viability of the establishment, for it ensured ready access to travelers. As Brown discovered, it also provided a quick and easy escape route for those with such a need. It was at Menefee's that he witnessed a deadly scene of frontier bloodshed.

The roadhouse was crowded one night, full of miners, trappers and a collection of various frontier lowlife, all seeking protection from the inclement weather. The chinked log structure was still in its rawest form, yet to be divided into rooms or graced with windows. Light was thrown into the artificial cavern from a blaze that was raging in a fireplace set into a far wall. A few odd candles melted on shelves and crudely constructed tables, casting the patrons in flickering hues of red and yellow. At one table, a professional gambler from San Francisco, Gilchrist by name, was dealing the cards for a game of Spanish Monte. The stakes were small, though, because the miners had more time than money at this time of year.

As the men huddled over their cards, a $20 gold piece was thrown on the table. Like corks firing from champagne bottles, all eyes popped upward. Upon discovering the identity of the newcomer, Gilchrist drew his revolver, an action mirrored by the stranger. These men were smooth, well practiced at the art of gunplay. Those around the table, Brown included, hit the floor with all the speed and grace of falling rocks. The stranger fired first, but missed. Gilchrist's revolver was the next to smoke, but at the crucial instant someone jarred his arm and the bullet flew wide of its intended target. The hot lead drilled a third eye in the forehead of a young English bystander. The poor man wasn't even aware of the dispute, and his ignorance proved fatal. In all the commotion that followed, the stranger disappeared into the night, never to be seen again. The story made better sense when Gilchrist later explained that the two were enemies from way back. They'd had a disagreement over a card game and a hotly disputed $20 gambling debt and had vowed to kill each other upon their next meeting. Gilchrist told authorities that the young man's death had been an accident, but he still found himself sentenced to time in jail.

With his supply of cash evaporating, and perhaps shaken by the unexpected violence, Brown jumped at another job opportunity as soon as it presented itself. He had heard that there was money to be made in furs, so he partnered up with another fellow and set out to trap marten. What money there was in trapping was linked to the Hudson's

Bay Company. The foundation of the HBC's operations was what might be called the freelancer. The company didn't employ its own men as trappers; rather, it traded with Natives and anyone else who had a good product to offer. Trappers journeyed to the fort, or a more local post, where deals were struck and goods exchanged. Having finally reached the Cariboo, Brown was not interested in going back to the coast to trade. Therefore, he sold his trappings to middlemen. The rich, silky furs of the marten were in great demand, and Brown made some $3000 for three months' work.

At last he had enough money to make a go at mining. While Brown searched for a good claim, however, another job opportunity presented itself. And, because Brown wasn't a man given to slavishly sticking with plans, his life took a new and unplanned twist.

ᴗᴗᴗ

In his search for work, Brown discovered that his military service and experience on the Fraser came in handy. In the spring of 1863, he was hired as a constable for Wild Horse Creek, a mining town in the East Kootenay District in the southeast corner of British Columbia. The first miners into the region dubbed the place Stud Horse Creek, a tribute to a wild, magnificent and apparently well-endowed black stallion that many of them had seen roaming the area. The name, predictably, offended government sensibilities and officials swiftly rechristened the town. And as reports of the discovery of rich gold veins snaked their way back to the Cariboo, the local population multiplied dramatically. Within a matter of months, residents numbered well in excess of 5000 and the place buzzed with commercial activity.

Wild Horse Creek. In 1863 British Columbia experienced its third gold rush in less than a half dozen years. This time miners were drawn to the colony's southeastern interior around Wild Horse Creek in the Kootenays. Folks first called the town Stud Horse Creek, a tribute to the magnificent, spirited black stallion known by many to graze around the mouth of the creek, but the name was quickly changed to suit government sensibilities. Wild Horse Creek became a true boom town, its population exploding to 5000 within months after the discovery of gold. At peak production in 1864–65, miners reportedly extracted $1500 per man in gold each week. Such large amounts of precious ore proved magnetic to the criminal element, so Wild Horse Creek had its share of transient gamblers and even the occasional murderer. Rough and tough as the town was, however, Governor Douglas' judicial system, which included constables such as John George (Kootenai) Brown, ensured that the gold rush into the Kootenays was mostly a peaceful affair.

At peak production in 1864–65, individual miners on the Wild Horse Creek extracted more than $1500 worth of gold each week. Reports suggest that the creek paid better in that single year than any California stream ever did. As in most mining communities, not all residents chose to moil. Some, like John Galbraith, who set up a ferry on the Kootenay River, preferred to make their fortune serving the needs of the miners. Others focused on providing for the desires of the men. Occasionally, there were those who sought profit without toil, and such folks were not restrained by any moral reservations about stealing...or worse. Such practices required the services of men willing to uphold the law—or at least men less likely to break it. John Brown was one of those men.

Hard work and equally hard play characterized the mining lifestyle. Alone, or with a few partners, most of the miners spent long hours over many days engaged in back-breaking, muscle-tearing labor. The lucky ones were able to pan for gold. For their troubles they might get a sore back from days spent hunched over the river or a rocker, sorting out the dust and rare nugget from the wet dirt. Others had to dig tunnels or pits to seek their wealth. When these fellows came to town with their gold poke, they were ready to let off some steam. And there were plenty of establishments willing and able to provide the necessities required for boiling over. Brown's job as a constable required him to deal with drunks on a regular basis. For the most part, these folks needed nothing more than a night in the local jail to sleep it off. This hospitality served the drunks well—after all, there were many in town willing to relieve an unsuspecting miner of his hard-won stake. When Brown caught up with these sorts of predators, they faced much more than a single night in the hoosegow. But among Brown's greatest challenges was dealing with the men who tried to pass off fake gold as the real thing. To successfully handle counterfeiters required a good eye and even better courage.

One fine June morning in 1863 found Brown seated on a bench outside one of the stores that made up a block called Galbraith's Ferry. Brown whiled away many an hour there because it was one of the more active parts of town and a good place to keep up with the local comings and goings. On this occasion, he was chewing the fat with Yeast Powder Bill Benniston, a local miner who was given his nickname after he once tried to substitute yeast for gunpowder in his mining activities. Later, he claimed he'd been drunk, but there were those in town who figured he was just plain stupid.

"You hear about that foolish Frenchman up Lillooet way, Bill?" Brown asked.

"I've heared tell of more than a few foolish Frenchies," replied Yeast Powder Bill, "but none up at Lillooet."

"It seems this fellow, Cadieux by name, was making his way into Lillooet," Brown continued. "He was a trader, a successful one by the sound of it, and had five loaded pack-horses with him. A few miles outside town, he was stopped by a tramp. Just as the tramp began to introduce himself, a blue grouse flew out of the bush. The tramp quickly asked Cadieux for his rifle, claiming he was a good shot and that he would get a meal for the both of them. I guess Cadieux couldn't resist the idea of some fresh bird meat, so he gave the fellow his rifle."

Yeast Powder Bill chuckled. "I think I see where this story of yours is goin'."

"Yup, you got it, Bill," Brown sighed. "The tramp drew a bead on Cadieux and let the bird flap off into the woods. When the Frenchman realized it was a stick-up, he made like the grouse and darted off into the woods. Before he could disappear into the trees, though, the tramp unloaded a barrelful of lead into his back. Cadieux went down with the force of a miner's pick in full swing. The tramp then took the Frenchman's gold—and the best horse of the lot— before hightailing it out of there."

"Seems to me this place might be better off without a fella as stunned as this Cadieux sounds," snorted Benniston.

"Maybe so," agreed Brown. "But it turns out he wasn't dead. When he came to, he climbed up on one of the remaining horses and made his way into town. Upon hearing the story, the local constable rounded up 10 community-minded folk, who set out for the desperado. The tramp mustn't have been familiar with the territory because they caught up with him near a box canyon, where there was no way out unless he could fly. He abandoned his horse and began to climb. After he found good shelter behind some boulders, he took a few pot shots at his pursuers. They returned fire. Pretty soon he ran out of ammunition, and they took him in peacefully. He's sitting in jail, now, awaiting the arrival of Judge Begbie," Brown concluded. "No word on whether the tramp and that grouse were in cahoots!"

Benniston laughed. "An' when ol' Begbie gits ahold of this bandit, he'll wish he never got outta da canyon," he commented. Both men knew that Begbie tamed the frontier with his own brand of justice, and his well-deserved reputation for severity reached into every nook and cranny of the colony.

"Speaking of Begbie, tomorrow's the day, Bill," said Brown.

"Day fer what?" asked Benniston.

"Gold commissioner shows up," replied Brown. The commissioner represented the level of authority under Begbie. His main functions included the registration of mining claims and the resolution of mining disputes. "Here we are, deep in Kootenay country, miles from the center of British officialdom in this out-of-the-way colony, and this fellow keeps up his rounds with a regularity known only by those on a diet of prunes," added Brown, who had endured his fill of pompous officials in his army days. "The commissioner'll be checking on claims, making sure all are properly registered. No problem with yours, eh, Bill?" Brown asked jokingly.

"Now, Brown, don't be gettin' on like that," pleaded Yeast Powder Bill, who immediately hightailed it as soon the subject was broached. As Brown chuckled away to himself, he saw three strangers in the distance. His job demanded that he be aware of newcomers, and these three struck him as suspicious. While Brown's eyes were trained on the three men, who boarded the ferry and disappeared across the Kootenay River, Galbraith emerged from his store and came over to Brown.

"Constable, I'm afraid we've been duped," Galbraith began, as he handed Brown a small, bulging pouch. "Fool's gold."

Brown took the pouch in one hand and sized it up. "Feels about right," he said, gently tossing the bag. He untied the knot that enclosed the pouch and poured some of the contents onto his hand. "Looks real good, too. Nice nuggets."

"It's high quality, Brown," Galbraith replied. "That's why I took it, no questions asked. Later, when I got a chance to test it, I discovered it was mostly copper, with a little gold and less lead. A fine and crafty amalgam. I don't know how they gave it the realistic shape, though."

"I remember a case up on the Boston Bar. Seems some counterfeiters had taken to tossing molten metal from a great height to bang it up a bit and give it the shape of real nuggets. Could be the same method," Brown suggested. "Recall the folks who passed it?"

"They were strangers, three of them. Bought some supplies and paid for the lot with this," Galbraith answered, pointing to the pouch.

"One real tall and skinny like a pole? Missing a few fingers on his left hand?" asked Brown.

"That's right. The others were shorter than that one, about the same height. One had a messy red beard and the other had a scar across his cheek that was bent crooked like Wild Horse Creek," he added.

Brown nodded. "I'll take care of it."

This was an unwelcome turn of events. There was no telling how much of the funny metal the men had passed in town. And with the gold commissioner about to arrive, the whole situation would show Brown in a poor light. He made some inquiries and the next day discovered that the three counterfeiters were squatting in a small, one-room cabin just outside town. Brown made his way there and knocked on the door. No answer. Brown slipped his Colt .45 out of its holster and threw open the door. In the dusky interior he saw one of the men begin to move for a rifle resting against a far wall.

"That'll be the last move you ever make, partner," Brown snarled. "Reach for that ceiling, or your carcass'll be a lead mine."

Quickly calculating the odds, the outlaw evidently decided they weren't in his favor. He froze before Brown's cool demeanor and the even colder steel of his revolver. Brown tied him up. The other two made the most of the opportunity and escaped.

Catching only one of three outlaws was a pretty poor average for any frontier lawman. Once his prisoner was secure behind bars, Brown sought to rectify the matter.

He organized a posse to bring the other varmints to justice. Because the counterfeiters had burned a great many folks, there was no shortage of men willing to help bring them in and Brown soon had 15 volunteers. The outlaws had made their way northwest, out of the East Kootenays, likely hoping to lose themselves in the crowds that filled the Cariboo. But the fugitives were soon caught; while they were excellent counterfeiters, they were poor frontiersmen and didn't realize that men on the run had best enjoy their meals cold. On the first night of pursuit, the posse spotted the smoke from the campfire and quickly surrounded the pair, who willingly gave up. They joined their accomplice behind bars the next day.

Brown had matters well under control by the time the gold commissioner arrived. Dressed in a bowler hat and red leather boots, the official was as out of place as the high-class English accent that congratulated Brown for being on top of the situation. "I'd expect nothing less from a representative of the British Crown," he stated matter-of-factly.

While the three men awaited trial, Brown took a new job as a guard at the penitentiary in New Westminster. The story of the counterfeiters, however, doesn't end there. On Brown's recommendation, a young man named Hubble was hired as the replacement constable. The fellow was green, so Brown gave him some pointers before departing. He emphasized that under no circumstances should any more than one of the criminals be let out of the cell at any time. The advice fell on deaf ears, and one morning Hubble let all three men out for breakfast at once. One of the men slipped behind the young constable and put the mug on him. With the outlaw's arm tightly wrapped around his neck, the constable found himself at the man's mercy. The criminals stripped the young constable down, tied and gagged him, and left him locked in his own cell. Taking the law officer's money and gun, they made a quick exit. Because the jail was in a lonely part of town, the situation wasn't discovered until the end of the day, when a blacksmith was called in to free the beet-faced novice. The three criminals were never seen in town again.

ᏕᎧᏋ

The life of a penitentiary turnkey was not the one for Brown, and it was only a matter of months before he resigned the position. Without work, but with a sizeable stake, he finally began to moil for gold. He made his way back to his old stomping grounds at Wild Horse Creek, where he partnered up with four other men. Together, they bought a claim near the mouth of the stream. Brown selected the place because he remembered that it was the source of more than a few fine nuggets brought to town by gleeful miners. It did promise to be a good location because it provided access to dust and nuggets carried along in the currents of both Wild Horse Creek and the Kootenay River, and the best part was that the claim came cheap. Brown and his partners mostly exerted themselves panning for gold. They'd take turns operating the sluice outfit, but occasionally did some freelancing at the river's edge. It turned out that there was little profit in panning. The boys soon discovered that Wild Horse Creek was pretty well played out. With promises unfulfilled, they were soon ready to toss in their pans.

In those days, there was always someone else burning up with gold fever who was willing to take a chance on the slimmest of opportunities. It wasn't long before a group of Chinese came forward, anxious to buy the claim.

"How much you want for this claim?" asked the Chinese man who was apparently the leader.

"Well, we're thinking that a fine claim like this oughta be worth at least $1000," replied Brown, who had been chosen as the group's spokesman.

"You must be jokin'!" exclaimed his counterpart. "No big nuggets from here in months. We check."

"You didn't check very good there, boys," answered Brown. "Just wait here a minute." Brown walked over to a sack where he kept his belongings. He reached down, pulled something out and returned to the group.

"I'd say this is a pretty good-sized nugget," he suggested, holding up a golden chunk of ore about the size of a small egg.

"That is nice nugget," agreed the leader of the Chinese. Narrowing his eyes and cocking his head, he added, "But how we know it come from here?"

"Now look, do you boys think we're gonna be hoarding our gold?" asked Brown. "Do we look like silly old backwoods boys, happier with a bag of gold than a strong bottle and a good woman? No, sir. When we find gold, it's as good as gone."

The leader turned back to his group, and Brown listened to the men conferring in Chinese. His salesmanship must have been persuasive because the leader came back with an offer.

"We give you $250," he said.

"I guess you're still not quite sure," chuckled Brown. "Well, I don't blame you. There's plenty of crooks plying these rivers. I tell you what, make it $500 plus five horses and the claim's yours."

The Chinese again discussed the offer.

"We give you $500 and one horse—final offer," countered the leader of the Chinese.

"Done," agreed Brown, holding out his hand. They shook on it and exchanged the deed for the money and horse.

The Chinese headed into town to officially register their claim, while Brown and his partners divvied up their spoils.

"It's easy 'nough to cut the cash," said Griffiths, one of the partners, "but how're we gonna decide who gets the horse?"

"We're going to play some cards," said Brown. No self-respecting miner was without a pack of cards, which were often necessary to while away the time. Brown retrieved his pack.

"Here's 25 chips, five each. Stud poker. The one finishing with all the chips takes the horse," said Brown.

The game went on for some time because no one was anxious to risk the prize on a reckless gamble. By nightfall, however, only Brown and Griffiths remained.

"If you c'n beat my aces, the horse's yours," Griffiths grinned.

"Well, your aces will beat my queens," Brown replied, "but seems that the devil's with me tonight—I have the deuces as well." He tossed the pair of twos on the ground.

"Sunnuva bitch!" exclaimed Griffiths, whose smile had quickly disappeared. "If I ever seen a luckier man than you, Brown, I sure don't 'member it. By the way, I've been wonderin' where you got that nugget. We ain't seen nuttin' bigger'n chicken feed 'round here, let alone a chick's egg. You ain't been holdin' out on us, now, have ya?"

"Let me tell you boys, I'd wager that a chicken's egg is probably worth more than this," Brown said, tossing the nugget into the air and searching for a favorite Latin phrase to deal with the situation. "It's a souvenir of a gold counterfeiting case I was involved with some months back. *Caveat emptor!*"

Brown and the men then headed back to Wild Horse Creek, and on the way they discussed their future. They still wanted to try their luck at mining, but figured the Cariboo and the Kootenays were mostly played out. They settled on trying their luck farther east because they'd heard there was successful placer mining on the Saskatchewan River. So they made plans to head for Fort Edmonton, though not one of them knew where it was located. The men decided on one last hurrah in Wild Horse Creek before they departed. Agreeing to meet mid-morning the next day, the five split up to enjoy a final taste of the raw pleasures of the town.

Brown wasn't lying when he told the Chinese that he enjoyed liquor and women. He wasn't inclined to prioritize the two, so he headed to Buckly's Saloon, a local watering hole and brothel where both could be found in sufficient quantities and at agreeable prices. Brown played hard; by night's end, most of his stake was gone, but so were the frustrations of panning for gold. Calling it a night, Brown found himself walking down the main street, muttering curses to himself. The guilt was upon him. It was a familiar visitor; Brown struggled with demons throughout his life. His grandmother, Bridget Sophia, had made certain he knew the difference between right and wrong. The knowing and the doing, however, were two different things.

Out of money, and unwilling to bother any of his friends in town in his current state, Brown made his way out of town to a shelter he had discovered in a previous needy time. It was an old, hollowed-out tree, its best days long past. He climbed into the hollow and snuggled into the confined space, content as any forest creature. "Ahhhh," he sighed. "At least there's pleasure in knowing that conscience sleeps until after I've had my fun." But just as he was drifting off into a restless slumber, voices brought him back to consciousness. Opening his eyes, he saw three men gathered around a small campfire just a few feet away from him.

"You know, I'd heard Jews were cheap, but I never thought they'd be so dang stupid," said one of the men, expressing the widely-held prejudiced views of the era.

"They won't be cheap nor stupid no more. We took care o' that," replied one of the men, waving his revolver in the air.

"Yeah, and their gold, too," laughed another, tossing a pouch into the air.

"I guess dey thought the gold escort was just fer fun," said one.

Brown sat still. Without a gun, or even so much as a knife, he was at the mercy of the men. He eyed a fallen branch that might come in handy. As one of the trio moved, the light from the fire fell right on Brown's face. He held his breath and remained perfectly still. Brown knew from experience that desperadoes such as these were not to be trifled with.

"We covered plenty o' trail since we brought down our…bankers," one of them said with a nasty-sounding laugh. "I think it's safe fer us all t' get some shut-eye."

The others responded with grunts and nods, and the men rolled out their blankets. Their snoring soon drowned out the crackling of the fire and the other sounds of the night. Brown relaxed. Sometime later, long after the fire had died, he too fell asleep. When he awoke the next morning, the men were gone.

Brown made his way to the jail and told the recently appointed constable his story. The news of the crime had just reached town, and Brown was filled in on the rest of the events. The men had robbed and killed three Jewish men who were making their way to one of the banks in New Westminster. It seems the fellows wanted to save a few dollars and had therefore decided not to make the journey with the gold escort, an armed group of 25 men hired by the government to protect miners and their gold as they traveled from the interior to the coast. The escort played an important role because the mainland interior held plenty of

men whose gold fever manifested as crime rather than honest toil.

Brown eventually caught up with his friends, breathing a
sigh of relief that they hadn't set off without him. Wasting
no more time, they set their sights for the southeast and the
easy fortune they expected to find on the eastern side of
the Rocky Mountains. They had no idea as to the location
of Fort Edmonton but figured that with any luck they'd
stumble upon it. They knew the prairies were big, and that
finding their destination would take more than a little luck;
they just didn't realize that there was big and then there was
PRAIRIE BIG. They learned soon enough. As they disappeared into the mountains, Brown filled his companions in
on his late-night adventure. There was quick and ready
agreement that they should steer clear of any trios they
might see along the trail.

PRAIRIE ADVENTURES
1864-68

WHAT BROWN DIDN'T KNOW as he and his companions slowly made their way east through forest and mountain was that the prairies were on the brink of a transformation. Newspapers were filled with reports that included similar information and advice:

> The prairies are little short of stunning. The fertile soil of the parklands and the vast stretches adjoining the North Saskatchewan River provide excellent land for cultivation. Additionally, there are untold miles of arable land. High-quality coal is found in ample quantities. There is little doubt that the region is ideally suited for settlement. Palliser's description has made it abundantly evident that a curtain of ignorance has long cloaked our understanding of the region. Consider that curtain drawn, and see the prairies under the light of a new day. Those with ambitions can do much worse than cast their eyes west.

Change charged the prairie air that John Brown was soon to breathe. Until mid-century the great western region was believed, by those few who gave it any consideration whatsoever, to be a barren, unfriendly expanse. Outsiders saw it as suited only for those few forced to call it home: heathen Native groups, magnificent buffalo herds and a few self-sacrificing missionaries and lonely fur traders. The harsh and foreboding image was promoted by the Hudson's Bay Company's governor, George Simpson. When given the opportunity, Simpson painted the region as one ill-suited for settlement. The opinion was less an honest assessment than a carefully considered strategy designed to limit the disrupting presence of white settlers. Since the 17th century, the HBC had operated from the shores of the great northern bay, trading with nearby Natives. By the late 18th century it had established a string of trading forts along the vast network of rivers that flowed through the region and emptied into Hudson Bay. The permanent physical presence allowed the company to control much of the fur trade.

In the early 19th century, the Hudson's Bay Company successfully completed a hostile takeover of the North West Company, a competing operation that traded out of Montreal, after years of war-like conflict between the two companies. With the merger, subsequent HBC efficiencies gathered greater returns than had been seen in many years. Settlers presented a threat to the well-oiled trading empire built by the men on the bay. Their presence would only undermine HBC authority and profits; settlement was best avoided.

Even the will of a man as prominent, powerful and respected as George Simpson was inadequate to deter the westward expansion of settlers. When the HBC's interests collided with imperial will, the former was forced to give in.

Increasingly, that will was shaped by the North American political reality. The British government looked south to Washington; what they saw caused anxiety. An aggressive U.S. government was rapidly expanding its boundaries and clearly had designs on the vast, unsettled west. Although there was no question that Rupert's Land, as the territory was called, was under British control, sovereignty meant little with only a loose network of trading posts and without settlers or military in place to enforce it. Americans also began to view the land west of the Missouri River as something more than a desert, and decided it was fit for settlement. Over time, a similar sentiment regarding Rupert's Land slipped into British consciousness. A necessary first step was to determine the reality of the image. To that end, two prominent exploring expeditions were dispatched in the late 1850s.

Captain John Palliser of the Irish gentry led the first expedition. He had hunted in the West in the late 1840s, and his enthusiasm for what he had seen was enough to qualify the blueblood as expedition leader. Supported by such influential bodies as the British government and the Royal Geographical Society, Palliser's expedition, from 1857 to 1860, produced a lengthy and detailed report that carried great weight and was widely read. While he warned of difficult transportation problems on the eastern and western edges leading into the prairies, and of an arid belt extending from the United States into the southern prairies, his report was mostly favorable. He contended that north of Palliser's Triangle, as the arid region became known, the area was suited for both agriculture and stock.

The second expedition was mounted from the Canadas in 1857. Led by an engineer, S.J. Dawson, and a geologist, Henry Y. Hind, its report shared Palliser's favorable opinions. While Dawson and Hind also raised concerns about

John Palliser and James Hector. In the mid-1850s, Captain John Palliser approached the Royal Geographic Society in Britain with a proposal to explore the unsurveyed British/American boundary from the Red River to the Rocky Mountains. Enthusiastic society members decided to turn the planned excursion into a scientific expedition and the British government supported the venture because the Hudson's Bay Company was losing its domination of Rupert's Land. The expedition investigated the possibility of a road between Lake Superior and the Red River, and mapped out the plains south of the North Saskatchewan River and the southern passages of the mountains to the Pacific. Geologist and naturalist Dr. James Hector and magnetical observer Lt. Thomas Blakiston accompanied Palliser. The expedition's three reports showed that the road from Lake Superior wasn't feasible and that, except for an arid region in the southern prairies of Rupert's Land (Palliser's Triangle), the area was suited for both agriculture and stock. The reports became an essential source of information about the area from Lake Superior to BC's Okanagan Valley.

the farming viability of the southern plains, their conclusion was that the region's agricultural potential, on the whole, made it attractive for settlers.

These reports marked a change in how Britain and its North American colonies viewed the West. The cold, empty wasteland was suddenly transformed into a land of bountiful opportunity, and visions of profits danced in the heads of eastern politicians and entrepreneurs alike. To realize such profits two changes were essential, and both centered on issues of control. It was first necessary for Canada to achieve uncontested ownership. Political sovereignty was achieved in 1869, when the newly created government of Canada purchased Rupert's Land from the Hudson's Bay Company. This initial step cooled American territorial ambitions in the region—ambitions that a Canadian police presence, a railway and settlement would render untenable soon enough. The second change concerned the Native peoples. Their presence had to be addressed before any commercial exploitation of the West.

In the first half of the 19th century, the Natives on the prairies were still a formidable presence. Predominantly Ojibwa, Cree, Chipewyan, Assiniboine and Blackfoot, all but the last had adjusted themselves to the European fur-trading presence. Even into the late 19th century, the autonomous Blackfoot remained the most serious military threat to Canadian settlers. Relations with the fur traders resulted in differing degrees of cultural impact for each Native group, with the groups on the eastern expanses of the prairies most affected first. For example, by mid-century the Ojibwa had mostly abandoned the seasonal buffalo hunts of old; the herds had moved too far west and south for easy access. The Ojibwa were more regularly found employed as canoemen in the fur trade. As contracted laborers, they became increasingly dependent on the Hudson's

Bay Company for supplies, including food. With each passing year their hunter-gatherer lifestyle became more of a
memory. However, for most Native peoples, the great
upheavals that were to transform and often decimate their
societies still lay some years in the future. Generally, the
century that reached back from the 1870s was considered
to be the golden age of Plains Native culture; the introduction of the horse allowed for easier exploitation of the buffalo, and European traders presented a new market and new
supplies that together enhanced the lives of the people.

But if it was a golden age, there were dark clouds on the
horizon. In the first decades of the 19th century, changes in
patterns of buffalo migration and increased competition for
the humped back resource eventually resulted in a cata-
strophic impact on traditional Native practices and relationships. Under combined pressures from both the south and
the east, the vast buffalo herds were dwindling. By the
1850s, they were no longer the "oceans of brown" that once
rolled over the grasslands. American buffalo hunters, spurred
on by a U.S. federal government that saw the decimation of
the buffalo as an effective strategy for reining in Natives in
its territory, slaughtered the animals. The new presence of
the Métis, who made their living hunting the animals, also
dramatically reduced the herds. Dwindling herds had a striking impact on Native territorial patterns. To ensure continued access to buffalo, the Cree and Assiniboine were forced
west. These groups were the traditional enemies of the
Blackfoot, and their historically sporadic warfare was intensified with migration. The Métis also found themselves
under increased attack as they encroached on Sioux territory south of the international border. The Sioux did not
always passively wait for the arrival of the Métis, so bands of
Sioux warriors roving north presented a constant threat to
Métis hunters.

By the late 1860s, violence emerged as a powerful solution to the scarcity of buffalo—and, by extension, of food, shelter and supplies—faced by western Natives, and warfare became common. From all sides, Plains Native culture was under attack. Even when tomahawk was not raised against bow and arrow, there were other threats. Christian missionaries preached a new religion that often served to undermine or change traditional practices. Epidemics swept through the land, killing thousands of Native people who lacked immunity. Whisky traders from the U.S. delivered their own brand of death and destruction in the form of poisonous firewater. All this occurred against a backdrop of starvation and increasing poverty. As anxiety mounted over the vanishing buffalo herds, and as the threat to a people and a way of life became undeniable and immediate, Native anger intensified. Until peace came in subsequent years, with the arrival of the North-West Mounted Police and the signing of the numbered treaties, the prairies saw more violence than at any other time in their history

As the 1860s drew to a close, the Canadian West had changed considerably from what it had been a mere few decades earlier. Easterners saw the West as a cornucopia that would provide the economic foundation for a fledgling nation. Natives saw it as an ancestral homeland under siege. The vision of the former and the reality of the latter collided in the place that John Brown was soon to call home.

၅၇၁

As Brown and his companions emerged from the eastern end of the South Kootenay Pass in the autumn of 1865, the ravine gave way to a sublime vista. The party had stumbled upon a majestic site that touched the Irishman deeply.

Before them lay two crystal blue lakes, almost divided by two gently sloping plateaus of land that longed to touch each other. Looming mountains offered their benevolent protection. In the distance, other peaks reached high into the sky, some lost in the clouds.

"Boys, I have seen glories such as this only in my dreams," Brown declared. "This is the place for me."

But not yet. The weeks that followed their departure from the Kootenay district must have had a dreamlike, and occasionally nightmarish, quality for the men in Brown's party. Sure, they were headed for Fort Edmonton, but having a destination and knowing how to get there are two very different matters. It was easy enough to choose South Kootenay Pass as the initial step on their journey because it was one of the few accessible routes through the southern Rocky Mountains. Once they made their way through the pass, however, the travelers' fragile peace gave way to confusion and disagreement. In the increasingly heated debates, the vocal Brown always held his own. His style, however, was not one suited for achieving consensus, and as a result, his position was rarely adopted.

As the men made their way through the foothills, their doubts and concerns were rendered temporarily irrelevant by the sight that stretched before them. In an effort to get their bearings, the men climbed to the peak of a small summit. Gazing out over the prairies, they saw a huge number of buffalo moving as if one great mass. Reaching to the horizon, the herd seemed to stretch before them to all points of the compass. For Brown, who had never seen a buffalo, the encounter proved memorable. The men made their way to the edge of the herd, and brought down a young bull. For the first meal of many to come, Brown feasted on buffalo. Gorged on fresh roasted meat, the men considered how they might continue east in the face of this

South Kootenay Pass. Brown sensed that the Kootenays would become of great importance to him in later life. The trail through the South Kootenay Pass was well marked because the Kootenay Indians used it to drop down to their summer hunting grounds on the plains of present-day Alberta. The lakes that Brown and his party came upon are now named the Waterton Lakes and are in a preserve that, much to Brown's dismay, was eventually named Waterton Lakes National Park for Charles Waterton, an English aristocrat and naturalist who had never even visited Alberta. He would have preferred that the lakes retain their original name of Kootenay Lakes.

imposing obstacle. The solution proved surprisingly easy because the buffalo were a docile lot. As the travelers penetrated the herd, the animals parted, a sight reminiscent of the Old Testament flight of Moses and the Hebrews through the Red Sea. Rather than use a staff as Moses did, the men fired off an occasional shot and successfully made a lane wide enough for the five men and their nine horses—though doubts about the continued docility of the huge animals nagged them. If the herd were to close in, the men would be helpless and, like the Egyptians, they would drown in the onslaught. However, the disinterested beasts simply grazed as the men slowly made their way. Those buffalo on the western edges of the herd's range were perhaps not yet familiar with the destruction that the strange white creatures on horseback could bring.

Over the objections of Brown, the men continued to make their way east in search of Fort Edmonton. Brown contended that it made more sense to follow the mountains north. He was also reluctant to travel into Blackfoot country. Brown knew the Blackfoot only by reputation, through the stories he had heard in gold country. He figured that knowing the stories was about as well as he wanted to know the tribe. The Blackfoot were an aggressive people, more so than most of the other Plains tribes. They didn't take kindly to the white folks, who they encountered in increasing numbers in their territory. To his dismay, Brown got to know their displeasure firsthand as the party camped at Seven Persons' Creek, near present-day Medicine Hat, Alberta. While the men were enjoying a meal, a shower of arrows suddenly rained down upon them. Brown took one of the sharp obsidian points in his side; only the creative and painful use of turpentine, generously poured into the wound, saved his life. Before long, the Blackfoot war party tired of the game and departed—none too soon for the men, each of whom was certain that an encounter with St. Peter, or worse, was in his immediate future.

After surviving the Blackfoot ambush, the men had to deal with other obstacles, each equally harrowing in its own way. Packs of wolves—hundreds of them, according to Brown—ran wild. The men had no way of knowing whether the animals might viciously turn on them. Rattlesnakes were as common as the blades of prairie grass, and the party knew enough about snakes to be wary of their fangs. Unfortunately, it was all too easy to innocently stumble into a nest, where a painful death awaited. The South Saskatchewan River valley was at the time also home to hundreds of grizzly bears, which feasted on those buffalo unfortunate enough to be mired in mud while trying to cross the river. One look at a grizzly using its powerful claws to rip a chunk of flesh from a helpless, bellowing buffalo was enough to convince Brown that the massive bears were a force of nature best avoided.

Understandably, the party didn't want to remain near Seven Persons' Creek, but the old disagreements resurfaced and the men couldn't agree on a direction. The argument inevitably triggered Brown's temper, and away he went. In language that left little possibility for either misinterpretation or heavenly access, Brown revealed just how upset he was with his companions, blaming their poorly chosen route as the cause of his near-death. The easiest solution was for the men to split up, and they did. Three decided to head north and continue the search for Fort Edmonton without their hotheaded companion. Brown and the remaining man, whose last name was Griffiths, chose to follow the South Saskatchewan River east across the prairies. They figured it would eventually empty into either the Atlantic Ocean or Hudson Bay. Somewhere along the way, the pair felt certain they would reach civilization, perhaps even Fort

Garry (now Winnipeg, Manitoba). This predominantly Métis community was much talked about in Wild Horse Creek because Fort Garry was the last place where overland miners from the East could replenish their stocks before heading across the prairies to the British Columbia interior.

Unfortunately Brown's companion was without a horse because his mount had been killed in the Blackfoot attack. Brown had two horses, but one of them served as a pack animal and he wasn't inclined to abandon all his earthly belongings—and, more importantly, his ammunition—to ease his companion's plight. Instead, Brown made a bull boat (he likely learned about its construction and the usefulness of the craft from other travelers), an odd construction that was a common vessel on prairie waterways. The bull boat served the limited navigational needs of most of the Plains Natives, allowing them to easily ford streams or travel short distances by water. For longer journeys, however, a bull boat was an awkward, cumbersome craft.

The only materials required to build a bull boat were willow branches and buffalo hides. The pliable willow was shaped into a circle approximately two meters in diameter and entwined underneath in the shape of a basket, reaching a depth of about half a meter. Stretched over the frame was a single fresh buffalo hide, attached at the top with pieces of skin. As the craft dried, the skin pulled tight to the willow frame. During extended travel, the bull boat had to be removed from the water regularly to dry, or water soaked through the skin and sunk the vessel. The bull-boater sat in the front of the craft and needed a cargo of similar weight behind him for balance. Using a paddle as a rudder, he was swept along with the current—the craft couldn't be maneuvered upstream.

After constructing the vessel and filling it with as much buffalo meat as possible, Brown pushed his companion into the stream and bid him farewell. "Keep your wits about you, Griff," Brown called. "Lord willin', we'll meet up in Fort Garry"—if indeed the fort was somewhere along the river.

Brown continued on in a northeasterly direction, generally remaining true to the river's course. The vast, empty plains provided a stark contrast to his experiences across the Atlantic. Even after Ireland had been ravaged by famine and depopulated by frustrated emigrants, it was difficult to travel far in that country without meeting a soul. And there were no fences here on the prairies, so different from the home of his youth where each plot was parsimoniously marked with protective stone walls. As he surveyed the sprawling vista, Brown reflected on the monumental problems his grandmother had faced while seeking employment for him. Her inkwells ran dry with the letters she had written to authorities requesting an ensigncy for him in the British military. Here a determined man could live on his own; there, he depended on the whims of others. Riding in the crisp autumn air, Brown found great appeal in the cresting waves of brown grassland and the gigantic blue sky.

After some weeks of travel, Brown stumbled upon his first community. Duck Lake was a Métis settlement on the northern edge of the buffalo range. Prolifically treed, the area around Duck Lake provided ample shelter and fuel. The Métis who lived there were mostly from Fort Garry, and they used the location for wintering after a summer of tracking and hunting buffalo. There were about 50 families, all in good shape because the yearly hunt had just concluded. With winter setting in, the community extended to Brown an invitation to stay, which he gratefully accepted. It was his first encounter with the Métis, and he enjoyed it to the hilt.

Brown spent his first days learning the Cree language and hunting. One morning, while Brown was off hunting alone, a young Métis came running to him.

"Brown, Mr. Goldtoot' 'as arrived at da settlement!" the boy exclaimed, gasping for breath. "An' 'e says dat 'e wants to see you."

This was a puzzle indeed; Brown knew only a handful of men on the prairies, and certainly no one by that name. Abandoning his hunt, he hurried back to the settlement with the Métis lad, who took him to the mysterious stranger.

"Well, if it's not Griff!" said Brown, extending his hand. "I'll be damned!"

With a broad smile that revealed the gold tooth in the front of his mouth, Griffiths took the hand in his own. "Well, Brown, that bloody bull-boat contraption worked," he said, half in amazement. "When she was dry, she bobbed like a tub. But, boy, the smell was powerful bad," he added, laughing.

During the winter of 1865–66, Brown learned much from the generous Métis people, including a variety of frontier skills that would soon prove handy. With spring on the horizon, the two decided it was time to continue on to Fort Garry. Supplies in the settlement were becoming scarce, and the last thing they wanted to be was burdensome. With the snow still on the ground, Brown hitched his two horses to a sleigh he had built during the winter, and the two headed east. They crossed the White Mud River, and passed through Portage la Prairie and the Touchwood Hills. After six weeks, they made their way to Fort Garry, and none too soon as the runners on the sled were scraping bare ground.

∽∾

For all the talk of Fort Garry that Brown had heard back in British Columbia's gold country, the place itself proved less than imposing and perhaps even disappointing. The Hudson's Bay Company post at the junction of the Red and Assiniboine rivers was accompanied by only five houses. For the time and place, however, there was a respectable enough commercial presence: Mulligan's Boarding House, Beaucamp's Saloon and two stores. One of the local merchants had just imported photographic equipment, and Brown himself posed for the first tintype taken west of Red River. After mulling over the situation for about a week, Brown headed back west to Portage la Prairie on the Assiniboine River, about 100 kilometers from Fort Garry. His friend, "Goldtooth," decided that he had had his fill of the West and made for the settled lands of eastern British North America.

In many ways, Portage la Prairie was little different than Fort Garry. Though the community did not spring up around a Hudson's Bay Company fort, there was a fort nearby. The big shot in town was a Métis by the name of Sutherland, who owned a windmill, a trading store and a house—just about all the buildings in the settlement. Not too far off, Johnnie Gibbons also had a store. Charlie House, an American trader, did business there. A few folks farmed in the area, and a clergyman named A.C. Garrioch preached in the region. Once in Portage la Prairie, Brown set himself up as a trader, dealing west to the White Mud River, about 25 kilometers distant. His customers were mostly small, scattered bands of Chipewyan and Cree. Brown made no effort to establish a permanent presence. He purchased supplies from House, who, along with the HBC post and a couple of traders at the White Mud River, provided his only competition. Brown traded the staples. The Natives brought in muskrat, fox, mink, coyote and wolf furs; in exchange Brown gave clothing, blankets, beads, thread, tea, sugar and booze.

The Natives were good traders and generally drove hard bargains, at least until the whisky took control. It was rare

By the time Brown had this photo taken at Red River, photography techniques had undergone more than 300 years of evolution, beginning with the first *camera obscura* (dark chamber), credited to several men including Leonardo da Vinci. The discovery of light-sensitive salts by physicist Johann H. Schulze in 1727 was the first step in the development of early photographic techniques that saw French inventor Louis J.M. Daguerre (1839) expose a light-sensitive metal plate and then "fix" it with mercury vapor (the Daguerrotype). Later in 1839, British scientist William H.F. Talbot developed a negative to positive system that allowed for permanent images on light-sensitive paper. The technique used by Brown's photographer evolved from a process that used a glass plate dipped in a sticky, wet substance called collodion (wet-plate photography) to thin metal plates called ferrotypes (also know as tintypes) that held the solution. The plates had to be developed before the solution dried, so Brown may have had his photograph within hours of the sitting.

that a Native didn't want alcohol as part of any trade, and Brown soon discovered that the real money was made in trading whisky, which he sold for $30 a gallon. Whether he was already involved in plying the creatively mixed fire-water is unknown, but even trading the good stuff was enough to give him a bad name in the small and close-knit community. Because he was a newcomer who readily sold booze to the Natives, many of the disapproving pioneers labeled him one of the "Yankee Boys," a despised lot. And, as Brown was to discover, while the sale of whisky was lucrative enough, it came with real risks.

Brown was in the habit of bringing the furs he acquired at the White Mud River to Johnnie Gibbons' place in Portage la Prairie. One time he arrived to find about 30 Red Lake (Santee) Sioux from Minnesota also at the store. The Minnesota Sioux had a rotten reputation. Forced west by American settlers, who took their land and all too readily ignored treaty obligations, the Sioux took matters into their own hands in the early 1860s by waging war on the white settlers they found between Pembina and Fort Abercrombie. Eventually, the American Congress exiled some 10,000 Natives from Minnesota. Hundreds of them escaped by making their way northeast to the Red River region. While many of them sought the protection of Queen Victoria, the Great White Mother, they continued to carry the deep scars of the way they had been treated by the white man. With alcohol lessening any self-restraint they possessed, these Natives became a fearful and occasion-ally violent presence.

Because Brown could speak the Red Lake Natives' lan-guage, Gibbons persuaded him to stay for the day. Gibbons, with a reputation as a Yankee Boy, also dealt in whisky. There were no cups or glasses to use, so the small copper kettles provided by the Hudson's Bay Company served as

drinking containers. The common practice was for a Native
to bring in his furs and, with the trading complete, make a
request for his kettle to be filled as partial payment. With the
vessel topped up, he would either drink it on the spot or
make his way back to camp, where he would soon enough
dispose of it. On this particular day, it was Brown's job to give
each Native as little whisky as he would accept for the trade.
All this was pretty normal activity, and things didn't get out
of hand until the Natives ran out of furs before they had
quenched their thirst. Satiated or not, they were already quite
drunk when Chief Starving Wolf, known by the locals as the
Wolverine, made his way over to Brown.

"More whisky," he demanded, raising his kettle before
Brown.

"You have more furs to trade, Chief?" asked Brown.

"No furs. We did not get good trade for furs. Not fair.
More whisky," he scowled.

Brown knew that he was flirting with disaster and that
the wrong answer could quickly immerse him in a blood-
bath. He considered the Wolverine's demand. Under the
chief's glazed and glaring stare, he finally replied. "Listen,
my red brother. You know I am not a man who speaks with
a forked tongue. As a friend, I will give you one more
drink—but after that, you'll get no more."

Brown's offer defused the situation. The Wolverine took
his kettle full of whisky and departed.

Pleased with the day's trade, Gibbons asked Jimmy
Clewitt, a local old-timer, to go out to the supply house
and retrieve a gallon of the good whisky so that all the
white folk present could celebrate. Brown watched out
the window as Clewitt made his way to the supply house.
The young clerk, Billy Salmon, was afraid that ill might
befall the old-timer, so he also made his way out to the
supply house as a precautionary measure. Just as Clewitt

opened the door of the supply house, the Wolverine jumped in after him.

"Jimmy's in for it!" Brown shouted. "The redskin's after him, and he's got a gun!"

Brown's cry was followed by chaos. A gun went off, and the men saw Clewitt make a dash back for the store. Salmon followed him along with the Wolverine, whose kettle was again filled with whisky.

Clewitt fell on the steps of the store. "It's over for me," he moaned, prostrate on the ground.

"I'm shot!" cried Salmon, who collapsed on top of Clewitt.

The Red Lake Natives, using the supply house as a shelter, launched a barrage of lead at the store. The thud of bullets slamming into the log walls echoed through the building. That noise was joined by the sound of rattling and crashing store goods that fell victim to the occasional bullet that made its way through a window or an open chink between the ill-fitted logs. Brown, Gibbons and Bob Olone, Gibbons' cousin, took up defensive positions and answered the gunfire with some of the same. Revived, the wounded Clewitt threw Salmon's inert body off his back and stumbled back into the store.

The Natives who peered around the corners of the supply house to get off a shot were met with a hailstorm of hot lead. Simultaneous shots brought down one Sioux foolish enough to fully expose himself to Brown and Clewitt. The man's friend tried to drag him back to safety and got a bullet in the leg for his efforts.

"Boys," shouted Olone, "we're almost out of ammo!"

The men knew that without bullets they'd be easy pickings for the Natives, who were not known for their mercy. Their only hope was reinforcements. The closest settler was a Métis named de Marias, but he had to be made aware of the situation. All the men knew what was required. For a brief moment their eyes fixed on each other.

Finally, Olone made a break for the front door. "I'm off, boys!" he called. "Stand fast, I'll not be long." With a scream, he burst through the front door, his rifle ablaze. Without so much as a glance back over his shoulder, he soon disappeared from sight in the cover of trees.

An already grim situation took a turn for the worse. Brown and his cohorts were long past the point of being able to return shot for shot and were reduced to firing off the occasional bullet because only a handful of rounds remained. The men were certain that death and scalping was in their near futures…and not necessarily in that order. Olone had been gone for what seemed an eternity, and the men had just about given up on him when he returned. In truth, his efforts had only taken about an hour. Accompanying him were some 20 Métis and whites. When the Red Lake Natives saw the reinforcements, they scattered like leaves in the wind. "Whoopees" and "yee-haws" quickly replaced the sounds of gunfire.

They turned their attention to the two injured men, Clewitt and Salmon. Clewitt had taken the Wolverine's knife in the ribs and had pulled it out himself before picking up a rifle to return fire. All the doctoring he got was a plaster of heavily salted buffalo meat. It was medicine enough; within a couple of weeks, he was up and around again. Salmon wasn't so lucky. He'd caught a bullet and, try as they might, the men couldn't remove it. A doctor had recently arrived in Fort Garry, and the men decided to have Salmon sent overland to him. Afraid of possible Native attack, Gibbons hired an escort of six mounted men to see the wounded man safely there.

Back at Gibbons' store, the supply house store of whisky was broken open to celebrate the victory and the men were soon drunk. Inhibitions gone, one of the men—and Brown admitted that it might well have been himself— decapitated the dead Native. The butcher climbed to the roof of the store with head in hand and impaled it on a stick that protruded through the thatching. The gruesome souvenir remained there for several weeks, its long black hair and decomposing features an unmistakable warning to other Natives who traveled in to trade at Gibbons'. Apparently, there was little to distinguish Natives and white men when drunk.

Though the hired escorts tried to make Salmon's journey as comfortable as possible, the bumping and jarring of the wagon on the rough and pitted trail didn't do his frail health any favors. The young man was buried two weeks after the gun battle.

ᔕᖇᴄ

Following the violence with the Red Lake Sioux, Brown abandoned his trading enterprise and made his way back to Fort Garry. He was in search of new employment, preferably in an environment that did not give free rein to his wilder side. During the opening of the West, opportunity always knocked for those who listened. Brown, with ears cocked, had been in Fort Garry only a short time when a fellow came up from Dakota looking for men to ride a mail delivery route in the American territory. He was an agent of Charles Ruffee, a businessman who was awarded a government contract to carry U.S. Army mail between Fort Abercrombie, in eastern Dakota, and Fort Benton, in northwestern Montana.

Ruffee's outfit was modeled on one established in 1860 by Senator William Gwinn of California and William Russell

Upper Fort Garry lies at the fork of the Red and Assiniboine rivers, in the heart of what was the Red River colony. Established in 1822, the fort served as a Hudson's Bay Company trading post. When flooding severely damaged the site in 1826, Lower Fort Garry was constructed some 30 kilometers downstream. Under the pressure of increased management needs and supply demands from the local community, Upper Fort Garry was rebuilt in 1836. The fort's importance as a supply center and storehouse for points north and west ensured that the local community was a heterogeneous one, with high-ranking HBC officials alongside Métis and British mixed-bloods seeking employment. The fort took its place in Canadian history during the Red River Rebellion when Louis Riel's forces seized it late 1869. When British nationalists attempted to retake the fort later that year, Thomas Scott was taken prisoner. Scott was later executed by the Métis provisional government, an act that was to galvanize eastern English Canadian opinion against Louis Riel. Upper Fort Garry finally outlived its usefulness with the decline of the fur trade and the growth of Winnipeg.

of Russell, Majors & Waddell, the great American plains freighting outfit. Gwinn and Russell fashioned an operation that saw young men on fast horses ride day and night in relay form. Such a strategy allowed them to cover the distance from St. Joseph on the Missouri River to Sacramento, California, in 10 days. Few thought it was a bad idea, and plenty more wished they'd thought of it first. Nevertheless, outlaws, highwaymen, aggressive western Natives and the telegraph resulted in the rapid demise of the Pony Express, gone within two years of its historic first run.

Ruffee learned nothing from the experience of the original Pony Express. His grand scheme included two-man stations at intervals of about 70 kilometers and a mail schedule that ran three times a week. It looked good on paper, but whenever the riders came up against hostile Sioux, the impracticality of the plan was readily apparent. The station keepers were sitting ducks for the Natives, and the riders' safety was far from guaranteed even on fast horses. Irate Natives killed and captured many of the riders because they saw the express riders' presence for what it was: an initial wave of white settlers intent on taking over their land. Unable to effectively deal with this problem, Ruffee's vision failed to become reality. The route never even reached its assigned western terminus. In just over a year, the whole scheme collapsed into bankruptcy.

When Brown joined up, he was assigned a stretch that ran from Fort Totten, on the northern reaches of the Sheyenne River just southwest of Pembina near the international border, to an unidentified western location on or near the Knife River, perhaps Fort Clarke. The route was about 125 kilometers, and it took Brown 24 hours and he exhausted three horses running it. It's easy to imagine him roaring into places like Halfway Station and Snake Creek, long hair streaming behind his head and buckskin fringes

dancing, his hard-run horse hot and lathered. Quickly, the
transfer of horses was made, with only a moment for some
water to quench the rider's choking thirst. Jumping up on
the fresh mount, he was off again in the grandest tradition
of the Pony Express. Brown plied the route until the outfit
went belly-up; when it did he, like many others of Ruffee's
operation, was left with wages owed.

Fort Totten became the closest thing to what Brown
could call a home during these months. By all accounts, it
was an unappealing place. The fort's walls enclosed the standard military buildings: guardhouse, prison, saddler, mule
drivers' room, stables, company quarters, hospital, store-
houses and offices. Because each structure was built with
similar materials (logs packed with mud) and in a common
style, there was little to differentiate one from another, and
to an approaching visitor the fort appeared as little more
than a collection of large stables. Additionally, the palisades
surrounding the buildings, and the cramped manner in
which the buildings were packed together, gave the fort an
unpleasant, prison-like appearance. To boot, the complex
was poorly run. Drunkenness was common, and the commanding officer—also a drunkard—lacked the respect of
his men. The fort's saving grace was the vista provided by
nearby Devils Lake. In order to see the view, Brown had to
escape the confines of the imposing fort walls. Métis and
Natives camped on the stretch of land that lay between the
fort and the lakeshore. While the close quarters and
enclosed spaces surely made him itchy, the booze undoubtedly acted as an effective ointment.

This period marked the first time that Brown had lived
for any length of time near a stable Native encampment,
and the experience was no doubt revealing. In his previous
encounters with Native peoples, Brown had too often seen
them at their most fearful or their worst, on the warpath or

This oil painting by Conger (1890) after a sketch by Louis Vaelkner (1867) depicts the construction of Fort Totten. The fort was located on the northern reaches of the Sheyenne River just southwest of Pembina near the international border. The army began construction on Fort Totten in July 1867; its purpose was to protect communications between Minnesota and Montana. At the time, there was a great deal of tension between encroaching settlers and the Natives whose lands they were invading. The government felt it was necessary to protect these settlers from roving bands of Sioux that were becoming ever more hostile as homesteaders increased in number. Thus, Fort Totten was not only a station on the communications route, but also a haven for settlers when Natives attacked.

drunk. In this environment, he was able to observe their more representative daily activities. Their clothing was often ragged and old, and poverty was obvious. The hard winter rendered the Natives dependent on army provisions, a phil-anthropic or self-serving act that put considerable stress on the fort's limited supplies. The Natives' horses had suffered so much that they were unfit to be used for hunting. But even amidst such despair, the people's spirits were often high. Natives and whites alike enjoyed musical dances and performances. A popular form of recreation was a game the Natives called "billiards." Using poles about two meters long, with all but three bands of bark scraped away, the player's challenge was to throw his pole at a rolling wheel of stone. The player whose stick's center band fell closest to the fallen stone won the point.

Not all of the Natives in the region were so friendly, particularly in the area around the Knife River where Métis from Red River carried on a winter trade in munitions and alcohol with Blackfoot, Sioux and Cheyenne. It was illegal trade, brazenly carried on under the nose of an apparently impotent U.S. military force. Well armed and fuelled by whisky, this trio of particularly anti-white Native peoples let their displeasure turn to violence against the mail carri-ers. Joe the Spaniard was a rider who also worked for Ruffee's outfit. He was captured on a winter run near the Knife River by a handful of Santee Sioux who had spotted the smoke rising from his cooking fire. The Natives claimed that Joe was carrying mail from Fort Buford, and therefore he must be intercepted. Joe's pleas to the contrary fell on deaf ears, and the Santee set the dispatches aflame. While his captors were thus occupied, Joe drew his revolver, but the Natives jumped him and knocked him out with a sharp blow of a gun-butt to the back of his head. Little fun could be had with a senseless victim, so the Santee began pulling single strands of hair from Joe's beard. The sharp pain brought him back to groggy consciousness. The Natives forced the bloodied and suffering Joe to cook his few supplies for their meal, beating him even as he carried out the demand. Finally, they destroyed his travois, killed his dogs and took all his clothes except a worn-out antelope jacket. Joe knew that they were going to leave him to perish in the snow and, preferring a quick death to the suffering of prolonged exposure, he begged the Natives to kill him. As one obliging Native drew his arrow tight in the bow, another—his motive a mystery—stepped in to prevent the murder. They departed, leaving Joe to wander aimlessly back to the nearest army post, Fort Berthold. Joe's traumatized mind sent him in the wrong direction, and he soon lost consciousness. Only the goodwill of a passing band of friendly Gros Ventres saved his life.

Brown was not unfamiliar with such violence, but the anger of these aggressive Natives made them seem more hostile than any others Brown had encountered. Once some Sioux captured him just east of the Knife River. Again, the Natives' drunkenness fuelled their hostility. Their message was clear enough. They would intercept all mail and kill the American carriers. Marhpisskat, the chief, spoke in well-reasoned words that left little room for argument.

"Not many moons ago, the prairies were black with buffalo. But wherever white men go, the buffalo disappear. The death of the buffalo means the death of the red man," Marhpisskat said. "Look at you, in your warm new clothes. You are the friend of the buffalo killers, and they provide for you. Look at me, a chief, dressed in rags. For me, their enemy, there is no warmth and comfort."

Marhpisskat fell silent for a moment, considering what to do with Brown. Finally, he spoke. "You are familiar to us. We know you are from the land of the Great White Mother.

We will spare your life this time. But know that he who works for the Long Knives is no different from he who is one of the Long Knives. Should you be taken again, your life will be ours."

They destroyed Brown's dispatches and then permitted him to go on his way. The immediate result of Marhpisskat's reign of terror was that mail delivery ceased west of the Knife River until the spring of 1868, several months later.

With the collapse of Ruffee's outfit, Brown found himself out of work but he was not unemployed long. The military still needed to have its mail transported between forts, so it set up its own operation. Experienced riders were in demand, and supply was limited because many of the Métis riders did not want to continue working in an atmosphere of hostile Native opposition. Furthermore, because the Métis tended to be on good terms with their Native cousins and were known to abandon their work when the buffalo ran, the military viewed the Métis with suspicion and increasingly declined to hire them. Brown, on the other hand, had both the bloodlines and the skills the military desired. He was quickly hired to run the route between Fort Totten and Fort Stevenson, just above the Knife River, near the northern reaches of the Missouri River. For the first time since he had worked as a penitentiary turnkey, Brown found himself with a regular and guaranteed salary: $50 a month, plus rations. Brown took the job with open eyes. West of Fort Totten, all dangers were heightened. Brown's new employers were certain to make him earn every penny of his paycheck.

THE AMERICAN WEST
1868-74

ON THE MAP IT WAS PLAIN enough. Imagined by politicians and drawn by surveyors, the 49th parallel stretched across the great plains and split North America into two nations. But the long, taut thread divided more than the western expanses of Canada and the United States. It separated national visions. In the latter half of the 1800s, both countries were infused with the enthusiasm of expansion and exploitation. In the south, lawlessness reigned, and the bloody red line of the shifting American frontier was easily identifiable. Certainly, there were occasions when the smoking irons and feathered shafts of the American West fired north, but such violence was rare and occurred only during Canada's infancy. The fact is that the process of ensuring that the great southern plains would be American created a "Wild West" against which exploits on the Canadian frontier paled in comparison. John Brown came to know the difference firsthand.

The American West did not always lend itself to the more noble aspects of civilization, and violence often found

hearty welcome. It was the singularly fierce relations with
Native peoples that most colored popular perceptions of
the frontier and exacerbated the fears of those who chose
to go west. Through the middle of the 19th century, the
reports detailing these relations painted a bleak picture,
stark with details of terror. Variations on this bloody theme
dominated the reports that flowed back east and provided
the backdrop for American expansion. Frustrated and fearful settlers felt compelled to protect their homesteads.
"Patrick Connor and his associates kill 224 Bannock and
Shoshone near the Utah–Idaho border," read one news
story. Civilian violence often forced the military's hand and
it found itself acting as a buffer between the two parties.
However, the military was no shrinking violet. Realizing
the dream of an unobstructed transcontinental nation
meant that Native peoples would have to be brought under
control. "Colonel John Chivington and his forces wipe out
500 Cheyenne in Colorado. Many women and children
among the dead," read another report. Angry Native peoples proved unwilling to be passive victims and often took
the offensive, harassing wagon trains and killing isolated
homesteaders. "Apaches in New Mexico take advantage as
soldiers called east to fight in Civil War. Forty-six settlers
killed. Women and children taken captive." And, yes, there
was also peace, but a buried tomahawk did not etch popular consciousness as deeply as a gory one did.

As Americans came to see the promise of the western
frontier, a sense of urgency infused their expansionist mission. Visions of the West that were born in ignorance
eroded steadily as evidence gradually proved them inaccu-
rate. For decades, the plains that rolled west to the Rocky
Mountains were known as the Great American Desert. The
name accurately summed up popular sentiment, and few
dared to call the region home. With the 1859 discovery of

gold at Pike's Peak, Colorado, and Nevada's Comstock Lode, miners set the wheels of change in motion. As reports of moderate climates and fertile land filtered east, a second wave of settlers rolled west. Ranchers looked at the great plains and saw profits. Cattle brought in from Texas and fed on the grasslands of the midwestern prairies could be sold for five times the initial purchase price. With such money to be made, the great cattle drives commenced. The introduction of new and sturdier varieties of wheat, and the creation of technologies necessary to produce the crops, enticed a third movement of immigrants. Public lands were increasingly thrown open to homesteaders and made accessible by rapidly expanding western rail lines, and farmers gobbled up the soil like a plague of hungry grasshoppers.

As settlers colonized the West, scheme upon scheme unfurled in efforts to breach the continental divide. Western wagon roads were carved through the plains, connecting localities as distant as St. Louis and San Francisco. Speculators played on the hopes and dreams that accompanied settlers west. Freighting outfits and settlers alike rode the dusty trails, often to considerable prosperity. Contracts were offered for postal services, and these operations came to figure prominently in reinforcing the country's flanks (one manifestation of this trend was the Pony Express and its imitators). Railway promoters outlined plans that not only linked east and west, but also gave access to as yet untapped, isolated regions. Occasionally, they even began to lay track; the Union Pacific and Northern Pacific trace their origins back to this time. Even the Civil War of the early 1860s couldn't dampen the enthusiasm that characterized the westward clawing of Americans.

The march of the shifting frontier trampled on the rights of the Native peoples. Neither reservations nor ancestral claims provided adequate protection. Engineers surveyed, miners and farmers squatted, wagon trains rolled and hide hunters decimated the buffalo, all with little thought to the impact of their presence and activities on the Native tribes spread throughout the West. Federal troops were sometimes forced to drive overanxious settlers back, and the government occasionally purchased land from the Natives, often acquiring huge tracts for a pittance. More often, Native braves donned war paint and rode to defend their way of life. Despite their fighting the good fight, even warfare eventually proved futile.

In the northern Midwest region where Brown found himself, the Sioux were the most active Natives. In 1851, the eastern (Santee) Sioux signed a treaty that confined them to a narrow region around St. Peter's River in the Minnesota Territory. Aggressive settlement continued to hamper the buffalo's northern migration in the years that followed, and by the mid-1850s it was rare to see even a stray bull northeast of the Dakota Territory on the eastern prairies of Rupert's Land. This devastating development laid waste to the Sioux way of life. Angry, hungry and frustrated, the Sioux began to fight back. In 1854, a camp of Miniconjou Sioux wiped out 30 troopers who were seeking revenge for the Sioux's butchering of an immigrant's cow. In an effort to quell this disturbance, the government dispatched a cavalry of 1200 men, ostensibly to awe the tribes. They did more than awe. Using the white truce flag as a cover, General William Selby Harney's troops moved in on a Sioux camp at Ash Hollow and killed 86 men and women. The retribution apparently sufficient, the military promised to protect the Sioux's land rights. In future, no white settlers would be allowed to cross their lands, except in designated areas. The promise was predictably violated, and the military reneged on its pledge; the Sioux were left to fend off the intruders. Because the large numbers of Natives presented an imposing force, the Sioux were able to hold their ground for a few years without bloodshed.

Everything changed in 1862 with the eruption of the "Great Sioux War." In that year, government annuities to the Sioux were late in arriving. Traders were charging high prices and the encroachment of white settlers continued unabated. With motive enough, the Sioux found they also had opportunity when thousands of white men left the region to fight in the Civil War. The eastern Sioux acted, and the area around the Minnesota River was thrown into gruesome chaos. The bloodshed began when a small party of Sioux hunters challenged some whites to a shooting contest. When the settlers had exhausted their ammunition, the Natives turned on them and killed five men and women. Fearing government reprisals and seeking to cement his leadership, Chief Little Crow decided to throw caution to the wind. He took to the warpath. The ground ran red west through Dakota and south through Iowa. More than 800 whites were killed and hundreds more were taken prisoner. The army finally defeated the Sioux at Wood Lake. General Henry Sibley's forces rounded up 1500 prisoners, who were subsequently held to await punishment at Fort Snelling. More than 300 Sioux were sentenced to death for arson, rape and murder. President Lincoln later reduced the number to 38. Those who lived were marched to Nevada to face a prison-like future on a reservation.

The defeat didn't stop the violence. The following year, 300 Sioux were killed by a military force under the command of General Alfred Sully in a battle in northern Dakota Territory. Sully later met a force of 1600 Sioux near the Knife River. The Natives scattered under unrelenting cannon fire but continued to nip at the troop's flanks. In late 1866, another band of Oglala Sioux, led by Chief Red Cloud,

killed 82 soldiers as they tried to come to the aid of a group
of woodcutters who were pinned down near Fort Kearny.
The harassment provided by Red Cloud's braves was
instrumental in halting the progress of the Bozeman Trail, a
route designed to provide better eastern access to the gold
fields of Montana and Idaho.

This conflict between the Natives and the whites was
the setting for Brown's American adventures. As a civilian
employee of the United States Army, and a mail carrier, he
was among the vanguard of American civilization on the
Great Plains, a member of an organization that Natives had
reason to neither like nor trust. Thrown into the maelstrom
that was the settlement of the American West, Brown discovered the Native attitude at the feet of none other than
the great Hunkpapa Sioux chief, Sitting Bull.

ᔓ

Every cloud has a silver lining, and the violence that
pervaded the frontier also provided the opportunity for
Brown's employment with the American military. Brown
and a Métis named Joe Martin were hired in May 1868 to
replace two mail carriers recently killed by hostile Natives.
Brown and Martin covered the Fort Stevenson–Fort Totten
route, which sat right in the middle of Hunkpapa Sioux
territory between the Sheyenne and Yellowstone rivers. On
the morning of May 23, Brown and Martin left Fort
Stevenson with the mail. They were to meet the carriers
from Fort Totten about halfway, exchange dispatches and
return, as was their regular practice. But there was nothing
ordinary about this day.

Near Clear Lake, the attention of the two men was
drawn to movement in the distance. After some considerable

observation, which proved challenging in the heavy rain that had begun not long after they left Fort Stevenson, they agreed that the movement was a herd of buffalo and continued on their way. Soon they reached a narrow ravine, known as Dog Den, through which they had to pass. With a plateau above, many trees along the gorge walls, and Strawberry Lake off to the side hampering any easy escape, Dog Den was a well-known rendezvous point for Natives in search of victims. Brown and his partner cautiously entered the corridor, where they were suddenly ambushed. The two men quickly realized that what they had thought was a herd of buffalo had instead been a band of Hunkpapa riders, lying on the necks of their horses, expertly mimicking the animals for which they wanted to be mistaken. The flash of revelation came too late to avoid the attack.

To make matters worse, riding at the forefront of the ambushers was none other than Sitting Bull!

Although the Battle of Little Big Horn and the decimation of General Custer's men was still a few years away, Sitting Bull was already a force to be reckoned with. He had a price on his head in both Montana and Minnesota. With little to lose, he turned his band loose on the Dakota Territory, vowing to kill all white intruders—to him, a defensive strategy—whenever the chance was presented. His white enemies described him as a ferocious, hate-filled beast, but Sitting Bull merely acted on the truth that lay before his eyes. Since the coming of the white man, the ways of his people had been increasingly jeopardized and now existed under mounting threat of destruction. Those Natives who made peace with the invaders suffered the indignities of reservation internment, demoralizing poverty and belly-aching hunger. War brought Sitting Bull arms, ammunition, clothing and horses; it was good business, as he was known to say.

Sitting Bull was North American's best-known and most-feared native warrior. For many years he and his band of Hunkpapa Sioux harassed and attacked army camps and settlers to make it clear that whites were not welcome in Sioux homelands. In June 1876, eight years after his encounter with Brown at Dog Den, Sitting Bull won his historic victory at the Battle of Little Bighorn in Montana. Months later, Sitting Bull and his beleaguered band traveled to Canada assuming the Canadian government would protect them from a vengeful American army. But the Canadians perceived Sitting Bull's presence as both a financial and political liability so refused to provide his desperate band amnesty. After five years the starving Sioux had no choice but to return to America. Sitting Bull was among the last to surrender and eventually ended up in the Standing Rock Reserve. In December 1890, government officials ordered reservation police officers to arrest him because they were fearful of his influence over his people during the Ghost Dance. Sitting Bull was killed in the ensuing gunfight.

"Don't shoot! We are Medicine Bear's men," cried Martin in Sioux, citing the name of a Hunkpapa ally. "We are friends and travel in peace."

Sitting Bull sat atop his big gray horse. His appearance gave no indication of the reign of terror for which he was responsible. Portly, with two braids of long, tight hair and broad, jovial facial features, he hardly reflected the image of the Native warrior. He was quiet as he considered Martin's comments.

In the silence, Brown's packhorse, Lady Jane Grey, suddenly spooked and made a break for it. Brown's mount took off in the opposite direction. Whether he made use of the opportunity provided by the packhorse's exit to try to make his own escape, or whether his mount was just similarly spooked, remains unknown. Brown had lived through one Native ambush, and it's quite possible that he didn't want to push his luck. Sitting Bull glanced toward a couple of his men, pointed at the fleeing animals and whistled. The warriors took off in hot pursuit. When they returned with the fettered horse, they took everything from its pack. Brown's efforts also proved futile, and he was trotted back to the gathering under guard, his head hanging low.

Finally, Sitting Bull spoke. "On the ground."

One of the Hunkpapa excitedly slapped Martin's horse on the flank, and the band joined in a guttural ululating cry.

Fearing the worst, Brown and Martin found themselves subject to a cruel but common practice. They were stripped naked, all parts exposed to the elements. The Hunkpapa took their clothes and the remainder of their possessions. Sitting Bull then gave Martin an overcoat, but the "gift" wasn't a friendly gesture. Rather, the chief was playing a cruel trick. Brown and Martin silently identified the coat as having belonged to Joe Hamlin, one of the murdered mail carriers whom they had replaced. Two bullet holes were visible in the chest of the jacket, and two ragged tears in the back identified where arrows had pierced the fabric. Brown had already recognized one of the Hunkpapas' mounts as having belonged to Charley MacDonald, the other dead carrier. Sitting Bull's band had obviously been responsible for their murders.

In the background, a chant suddenly arose. "Kash-ga. Kash-ga. Kash-ga."

The two men knew that these words meant "kill them." Sitting Bull was not quite so anxious. "There is no hurry," he calmly suggested. "Prepare a fire, and then the fun can begin."

This suggestion did not indicate an improved turn of events. A quick death was preferable to the torture that Sitting Bull likely had in mind. While the two men tried not to give up hope, images of suffering crept into their thoughts. They might be buried up to their necks and left to die as a meal for insects. Or perhaps Sitting Bull had a more playful punishment in mind. They'd heard that the Sioux enjoyed sticking pieces of dry wood or pine pitch over a victim's bodies and slowly setting each one afire. Whatever the torture, the men were certain that it would end with their scalps being carried away as gruesome trophies.

"Who are you?" asked Sitting Bull. "What are you doing in our territory?"

"We are Métis, Sioux half-breeds from Red River," replied Martin, still speaking in Sioux. "We are on our way to St. Joseph to hunt buffalo. We are your brothers. Why do you rob us and talk bad words? Why do you want to do evil things to us?"

"Humph," grunted Sitting Bull. "We have just killed two half-breeds and a soldier. I would not have killed the men from Red River, but my men acted before we knew who they were."

"I killed one of them," said a Hunkpapa warrior. Brown looked at the brave, and saw that he was carrying MacDonald's Henry rifle. "I took him down with an arrow, and finished him off with his own gun as he lay on the ground," he explained, a devious smile cracking his face. "There was terror in his eyes."

Brown surveyed the band and noticed that some of them wore pieces of the carriers' clothing. His eyes shifted back to Sitting Bull and, for the first time, he noticed MacDonald's pocket watch hanging from the chief's neck.

"You are Sioux," Sitting Bull said to Martin. "But your friend looks to me like a white man. Are you Sioux?" he asked, pointing to Brown.

"My father was a white man, and my mother a Santee Sioux," replied Brown, hoping that his long dark hair would be convincing in the rainy twilight. Sitting Bull watched him, but Brown knew enough of Native ways to not meet the great chief's eyes, which was a sign of aggression. He held his breath, waiting. Finally, Sitting Bull spoke.

"Your skin is pale, and your eyes are blue, but you speak good Sioux. You may well be a half-breed. But if you are our brothers, why do you help our blood enemies, the *isa thonga*?"

"We do not help the Long Knives," replied Brown. "We are but poor hunters. On our way to St. Joseph, we stopped at Fort Stevenson. The commander offered us money to carry these letters to Fort Buford. It was for one time only, and the few dollars were important to us."

Sitting Bull rode away from the men and held council with his braves a short distance from the prisoners. A loud and rancorous dispute broke out over how the men were to divide the spoils.

"I'm not sure what their plans for us might be, Joe," muttered Brown, "but I think we best make a break for it."

"If we do, they'll shoot us," replied Martin. "But hell, that beats being burned alive."

Buck naked, the two men fell to the ground, rolling like logs, making slow and quiet progress. They traveled for some 30 meters, eventually tumbling into the coulee that reached to the shores of Strawberry Lake. Then the two men stood and, muddied black as pitch, ran for the water. The lake's edge was overgrown with bulrushes and weeds, and the escapees took cover hoping the lake growth would provide adequate shelter. They weren't in the water long when they heard the roar of their captors. In a matter of minutes, the Hunkpapa were at the edge of the lake.

The braves fired blindly as they ran up and down the shore. Their targets were small, though, because Brown and Martin stood up to their necks in murky water. The heavy wind and torrential rain muffled the Natives' shouts. They soon gave up, and, assuming the men must have escaped, made for the trail. The two men remained in the water for another half-hour, until the cold forced them out. Numb, they began to make their way back to Fort Stevenson, avoiding the main trail until they were a few kilometers away from Dog Den.

"The trail'll be safe now," said Martin, and they moved onto it.

With daybreak, the men surveyed their surroundings. As they looked back along the trail, they discovered that Hunkpapa were still visible, so they darted back into nearby ravines. Still as naked as Adam before the apple, the men proved to be a fine meal for the multitude of mosquitoes that swarmed in the warm morning sun.

Fort Stevenson appeared on the horizon in the early afternoon. A sentry soon spotted the two men and made his way to the sergeant of the guard.

"Sir, two Injuns is approachin' from the west. I think, sir, that they's...nekkid," he reported.

The sergeant left to capture the two men, fully expecting to find two drunk Natives. As he approached the fugitives, he recognized them. "It's not quite that hot today, boys," he joked. "What happened?"

"Not much," replied Brown sourly. "The Sioux got our mail, our horses, our clothes—and they almost got us! We just walked here from Strawberry Lake."

Their feet and bodies muddied and bloodied, and still without clothing, Brown and Martin were marched right to the office of the fort's commander, Philippe de Trobriand. The brandy flowed freely as he questioned them on the events of the past day.

"Those damned savages! MacDonald and Hamlin were young men, their lives unwritten parchment. MacDonald has a wife and three children, for God's sake. I've given a great deal of thought to the nobility of these people, but as heaven is my witness, events such as this prove that the redmen have no place in a civilized world! Every last one of them should be hunted down like the beasts they are. And they would be, if this cheap and nearsighted government would unshackle its forces and give us the manpower we need!"

De Trobriand continued on for some time, cursing the U.S. government in the sort of colorful language associated with the barracks and not the typically restrained vocabulary of the officers' quarters, for permitting such hostilities to continue.

Feeling lightheaded as a result of the good liquor acting on his empty stomach, and exhausted after his ordeal, Brown suggested that it was a good time for the two men to return to their quarters. De Trobriand agreed and sent them on their way. Doctored, fed and clothed, Brown and Martin fell into a deep sleep that lasted well into the next day.

ᏕᏘ

The encounter with Sitting Bull and the Hunkpapa was incentive enough for Brown to seek a change of pace. When the opportunity arose, he quickly opted for the better pay and security provided by storekeeping. Skills Brown had acquired while he was a trader in Portage la Prairie were of value during the fort's busy supply months of summer and late fall of 1868. While thoroughly engaged in keeping track of the flow of supplies, Brown called Fort Stevenson home. It was a new post, still uncompleted when Brown lived there. Built to replace Fort Berthold, located across the Missouri River, Fort Stevenson served as a central supply depot for the nearby army posts. Managing the supplies must have caused Brown no end of headaches because the fort simply didn't have enough storage capacity for all the goods that made their way through. And with the confusion of ongoing construction, running a store proved a somewhat stressful undertaking that demanded much more than simple record keeping.

Situated on a plateau, Fort Stevenson was framed by rolling hills, the narrow Douglas Creek and the mighty Missouri River. As a central administrative post, it was an imposing military presence in the region, with a garrison of 220 men and 40 civilians. Brown was a contracted employee. Buildings consisted mostly of the standard military structures, but unlike other forts, there was also a district commandant's house that reflected the post's administrative function. It was a large unit, consisting of seven rooms that were shared with other officers. Its structure was little different from the other buildings in the fort; it consisted of split logs, the chinks of which were filled with mud and wood chips. The roof was covered by hay and mud, which provided a pleasant enough insulation. Still, winter's successive freezings and thawings

This is a pencil sketch by Phillipe Régis Denis de Kredern de Trobriand of Fort Stevenson, April 1869. Built in 1867 along with Forts Totten and Ransom and located on the east bank of the Missouri River above the mouth of the Knife River, Fort Stevenson was built of neat, single-story adobe buildings. Like Totten, Fort Stevenson was an important point along the Fort Totten Mail Route. By the time the fort was built there were many calls for peace between whites and Natives, a peace that many whites believed would come only with the extermination of the Native peoples. But cooler heads prevailed and, in 1868, a peace commission was established to find a humane solution to the "Indian Problem." This commission was charged with getting the tribes to set-tle on reservations far away from where the whites were settling and traveling. The Treaty of Fort Laramie established the Great Sioux Reservation. Representatives of many tribes signed the treaty but it was hotly contested. In time, the U.S. government reneged on the terms of the treaty and it was renegotiated, but not to the satisfac-tion of the Sioux tribes.

brought problems when mud fell from the ceiling and small pebbles came loose and clattered to the ground, providing a constant, irritating background noise. The commandant even complained that hidden cracks in his bedroom resulted in regular snowfall. A corral, granary and sawmill were built outside the palisade, and a garden provided fresh onions, potatoes, peas, carrots and corn. Before the protective fence was built, soldiers, workers and friendly Natives wandered through with considerable freedom, greatly animating the place. Once finished, however, the site was well fortified. An alarm bell was ready to sound if more than one or two suspicious-looking Natives approached. Loopholes in the palisades and overlooking turrets ensured there was little opportunity for successful attack by any hostile parties.

Despite the work involved in storekeeping, the summer provided Brown with a variety of recreational opportunities. For what was likely the first time, Brown was exposed to American Independence Day festivities. At reveille, the fort was roused with the military band's renditions of a variety of national airs. Throughout the day the men took part in a number of different competitions, including target shooting and foot and sack races. Brown was an accomplished shooter and fleet of foot, and he certainly would have enjoyed the contests. At noon, a 37-gun artillery salute was offered. On this occasion, the celebrations were enhanced by the arrival of the paymaster, who made good the previous two months' wages. A rare wedding of civilians was also celebrated later in the month. Events such as these provided welcome breaks to the tedium of garrison life.

The winter of 1868 saw Brown again carrying the mail, an outdoor job more suited to his adventurous inclination. This time he was placed in charge of the riders, the increased responsibility a mark of the military's confidence in his ability. As chief carrier, Brown generally overlooked unofficial army policy and hired Métis because they possessed the sledding skills necessary for winter delivery. The sleds were simple vehicles, little more than a long board curved upwards in the front. Each unit was covered in a buffalo skin, much in the fashion of a bull-boat, and the driver sat comfortably enough on the mail and kept warm under a buffalo hide. The load was pulled by three animal teams, harnessed with a padded collar worn on the shoulder. Half dog and half wolf, the beasts that pulled the sleds were known for strength and endurance—*not* for friendliness. While teams could typically travel about 100 kilometers in a day, those on the Stevenson–Totten run were only expected to go about 60 kilometers.

The route was marked with five stations, built under Brown's supervision, which provided nightly shelter. On the third day of travel, carriers from Fort Stevenson met those from Fort Totten at the halfway station and, after an exchange of the mail, they returned. Ideally the whole operation took six days, but in winter weather, the ideal and the real rarely coincided. As Brown was to discover, venturing outside the palisades while snow covered the ground was always risky.

Occasionally the risks occurred when Brown served the military in other capacities. In March 1869 Brown was given the task of guiding four men to Fort Totten. The men had already tried the journey without a guide, but were forced to return, frostbitten by the −18°C weather. They apparently learned little from the experience, because they were ready to try again just a few days later. Though it was a clear day, the thermometer read −28°C. Brown objected to departing under such conditions, but pressure from the men forced his hand. All went fine until they were a couple of days' ride from Fort Totten, near Big Coulee. The day began crisp and

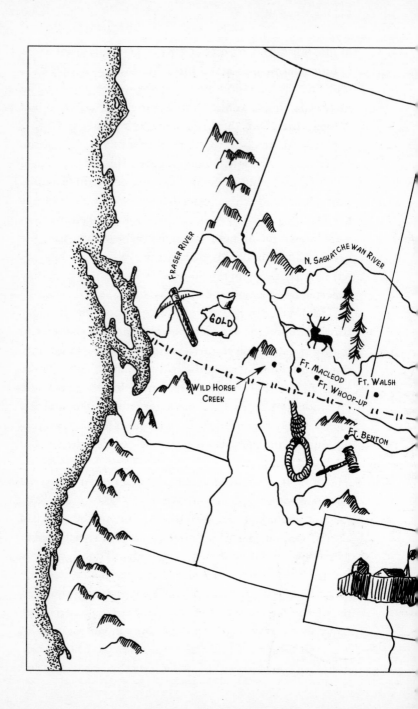

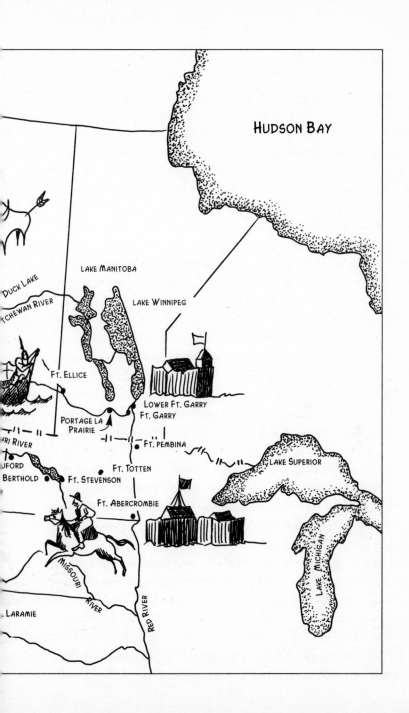

HUDSON BAY

LAKE MANITOBA

LAKE WINNIPEG

DUCK LAKE

TCHEWAN RIVER

FT. ELLICE

LOWER FT. GARRY
FT. GARRY

PORTAGE LA
PRAIRIE

RI RIVER

FT. PEMBINA

LAKE SUPERIOR

UFORD
BERTHOLD

FT. TOTTEN

FT. STEVENSON

FT. ABERCROMBIE

LAKE MICHIGAN

MISSOURI

RIVER

RED RIVER

LARAMIE

bright, but by afternoon it turned violent. A snowstorm suddenly blew in from the north, its ferocity new to Brown's experience. He ordered the construction of a snow house, but in the face of raging winds and blowing snow, a poor job was done of building it. The party suffered from cold and cramped quarters throughout the night. The next day was calm enough, but as the men emerged from their shelter, their wet clothes soon froze solid. Brown was forced to use one of the sleds as tinder. In the process of starting a fire, he froze his hand. The party somewhat warmed, Brown decided it was time to continue.

By this time, painful snow blindness had set in and Brown was unable to figure the appropriate direction for the group to take. He guessed that a timber stand was nearby. The depth of the fresh snow was such that the sleds were useless and they were abandoned. Continuing on horse, the party soon separated, and Brown found himself accompanied by only one man. Failing to find the stand, Brown and his companion tried to return to the sleds. On the way, they encountered another member of the party, who had disagreed with Brown's assessment of their location. He told Brown that the other two men had set off in another direction. He soon talked Brown's companion into attempting to follow the other two men. Brown continued back to the sleds alone. Soon after he arrived, one of the men also stumbled back to the sleds. The other had fallen behind, and conditions were such that Brown did not feel the risk of searching for him was justified. For three days they remained, burning the wooden sleds and making do with the warmth provided by the buffalo robes that the other men had inexplicably left on their departure. Still, the pain from the cold was intense and was only magnified as their fuel supply depleted. When the weather cleared, the pair retraced their steps to the Big Hollow mail station, where they were soon found by the mail carriers. Some 10 days after the initial storm, and 15 days after they left Fort Stevenson, the two men finally arrived at Fort Totten. Brown's frostbitten hand and left foot were severely damaged, but his fate was better than that suffered by three members of the party, only two of whose bodies were subsequently recovered. One of the dead men was discovered holding forged discharge papers, probably the reason for his urgent and ill-considered desire to leave Fort Stevenson. The military absolved Brown of all responsibility for the disaster.

For the next five years, Brown worked more or less continuously for the United States military, hired intermittently as a carrier, a guide and an interpreter. These activities were all to Brown's liking because they afforded him opportunity to be out in nature, in the environment he so fully enjoyed. He operated a twice-monthly military express between Fort Buford, about 130 kilometers west of Fort Stevenson, and Fort Totten. He later served as a guide for prominent military officials. On one such occasion, he was selected to guide Major W.S. Hancock on a tour of the region surrounding Fort Buford. The assignment took him to Pembina, a mostly Métis community near the international border. There he met and, in September 1869 after a swift courtship, married an attractive, young, local Métis woman named Olive Lyonnais, whom Brown took to calling "Olivia." They settled at Fort Totten, where Brown continued to operate his mail express, so that they could be closer to her family. To the military's dismay, Brown soon filled his carrier ranks with Métis men. Brown felt that these men's experience on the plains, and the fact that they had become his relatives, carried more weight than the military's view that the Métis were an undisciplined and transient lot.

When his mail contract expired, Brown found employment as a guide and interpreter at Fort Stevenson. While
there, he led an armed escort in search of a wagon train that
was lost somewhere northwest of the fort. The successful
search party was gone for nearly three weeks.

And around this time Brown also had another encounter
with the Sioux.

ᔕᔕ

"Giddyup, dogie!" shouted one of the cowboys as he
rode hard toward a steer that wanted to follow a path of its
own. When he was close enough, the cowboy gave the roving steer the butt end of his bullwhip and brought the beast
to its knees. The animal slowly regained its footing and
resignedly made its way back to the herd. There was no
place for independent-minded cattle on a drive, and those
beasts imported from the East seemed to have the hardest
time figuring that out. The cowboys were experienced,
though, and they kept the animals moving. This was Sioux
country, no place for delays. Because of that fact, the cowboys weren't alone on this job.

The few hundred head of cattle had to be trailed from
Fort Stevenson to Fort Buford. The Hunkpapa and Oglala
were still active in the region, and their view of the intruders hadn't changed; if it was white and it moved, it had a
good chance of seeing the business end of an arrow. The
military was acutely aware of the danger and, as a preven-
tive measure, had charged a full company of American
infantry, 100 strong, with protecting the cattle and the men.

Brown was entrusted with ensuring that the party didn't
get lost on the open prairie, and getting lost was all too easy
because there was no trail to follow. Brown liked scouting

work. He was well qualified for it because his years spent
working as a mail carrier had given him a good understanding of the territory. And a scout didn't have the same worries
as a carrier. A lone rider was an easy target and, if he was carrying mail, a likely one, too. A scout might be sent ahead of
his party to reconnoiter, but he always knew that there were
others on whom he could rely. On this occasion two other
guides, who served under him, joined Brown. They were
Jimmy Richmond, a Scot, and George Kipling, a Métis. The
unique drive had all the markings of a military undertaking.
The foresight proved to be warranted.

As the men rode, a bluff gradually came into view to the
east of the party. Great care was necessary whenever a natural obstacle such as this presented itself, because one never
knew what might be hiding on the other side. As the soldiers kept watchful eyes on the ridge, three Natives on
horseback appeared in full view on the crest. The commander immediately rode over to Brown.

"You boys catch up with those redskins," he ordered.
"Find out whether they're friendly or hostile. Assume the
worst."

Brown and his men immediately rode in the direction of
the crest. From a distance, it was impossible to tell what the
onlookers' intentions were. Maybe they were local Natives
who weren't on the warpath…not likely, but maybe. If so,
they could continue on their way. If not, they'd spend some
time housed at the expense of the state. When the braves
saw the trio coming, they vamoosed, but they did a poor
job of making their escape and rode into a blind coulee.
The steep hills prevented them from climbing out, and the
rapid approach of Brown and the guides meant that they
couldn't retrace their steps. Their options limited, the
Natives abandoned their horses and ran for the shelter of
some cottonwood trees.

"Why do you chase us?" called one of the braves. "We have not hurt you."

"Well, they're Hunkpapa," Brown said to Kipling after he heard the question. "Better be careful, boys." Then, shouting in the direction of the cottonwood trees, he said, "Why don't you fellows come on out so we can talk about it?"

"We will not come out," came the reply. "We are afraid of you."

"Now, you fellows have got no reason to be afraid of us. You come on out. The Chief Soldier of the whites is with us. He's got some grub and tobacco to give you," Brown added, laying it on thick.

After a moment's silence came the reply: "We want nothing from him. Leave us."

"These Hunkpapa are a proud lot," Brown said to Richmond.

"Too proud for their own damn good," Richmond replied.

"I don't see this coming to anything but a bad end, boys," muttered Brown.

As they were talking, the commanding officer rode up.

"We've got a predicament here, Major," said Brown. "Not a doubt these are hostile Sioux, and they're not coop-erating. If they escape, they're liable to gather reinforce-ments and attack us first chance they get."

"Let's see if a show of force will change the redskins' minds," the major suggested. He rode off toward the herd and soon returned with 25 soldiers. As a group, the men slowly made their way toward the cottonwoods.

"Damn it!" muttered Brown. "The buggers have block-aded themselves in that small cave. It's going to be tough to get them out of there."

"Who speaks the best Sioux?" the major asked Brown.

"Kipling, sir."

"You ask those redskins to surrender, Kipling," ordered the major. "Tell them that they'll be prisoners, but that no harm will come to them."

Kipling relayed the message.

"No. We stay," came the immediate reply. "We know you will kill us. But we have heard that the Long Knives are brave. Come and get us—show us you are brave."

Not liking the well-protected defensive position of the Sioux, the white men readily declined the invitation—all of them except Kipling.

"Major, let me ride in on those damned redskins," Kipling pleaded. "I'll make quick work of them."

"You certainly will not," the major retorted. "Brown, any ideas?"

Brown rubbed his chin and considered the odds. "Well, we could burn 'em out, Major. Set a prairie fire."

"A fire might do the trick, all right," agreed the major. "But if the blaze gets out of hand, it might burn all the way to Stevenson. And if that happens, there will be nothing left for the cattle to graze on."

Suddenly, the quiet was interrupted by a wail. All eyes were drawn to the dark entrance of the cave. The Sioux had begun their eerie death song. The soldiers fell silent as they listened to the chanting as it echoed in the coulee. This was not good news for the major and his men. It meant that the braves had decided that there was no way out, and that they were ready, and willing, to die.

The major's response was immediate, "Let's show them we mean business, men. Shoot their horses."

Because they were easy targets, the animals were quickly slaughtered. While the soldiers' attention was focused on carrying out their bloody order, Kipling made a break for the Sioux. When he got about 20 meters from their stronghold, a bullet to the forehead brought him down.

"Damn! Fire at will, men!" the major commanded, his jaw clenched in anger.

Bullets rained down on the Sioux position. Brown's party was met with defiant calls and a return volley of gunfire. Amidst the flying bullets, one of the braves ran for Kipling, took the dead man's gun, and squeezed off a couple of shots. He must have had a powerful spirit protecting him because he wasn't hit by a single bullet.

The gunfire continued. After hundreds of shots had hit the dark cave entrance, the major ordered a cease-fire. There was silence from the Sioux position—no cries, no return fire.

"Brown," the major barked, "you and Richmond go in there and see if they're still alive."

The pair slowly picked their way toward the hole. As they reached the entrance, they allowed their eyes to adjust to the darkness. They could see in the dim light that the three braves lay motionless on the ground. Still suspecting possible treachery, they trained their rifles on the Sioux and jumped inside with a yell. The Natives were dead all right.

Brown went back to the entrance. "It's okay, boys, they're goners," he called to the men. "Come on up!"

"Brown, I'm gonna take me a souvenir of this little adventure," said Richmond, as he unsheathed his knife. "I'm gonna take me some of this fine, black hair. Nothing that a Sioux wouldn't do!" he chuckled. Richmond opened the knife and grabbed one of the fallen braves by the hair. He pulled the handful tight toward the fallen man's back. As he put the steel against the brave's forehead, the Native's eyes opened.

"This sunnuva bitch ain't dead!" he shouted. "Cripes, the redskin's tryin' to bite me!"

Richmond slashed the man's throat to make sure he'd never bite again. Then he finished the grisly deed. When the men stepped out into the sunlight, they left behind three hairless Sioux. Before they made their way out of the coulee, they stopped to cut some willow. Green and freshly peeled, the flexible wood made a fine brace on which to stretch and dry a bloody scalp.

The rest of the drive was uneventful. A few days later, the men were safely inside Fort Stevenson, protected by its array of howitzer guns. Offers to purchase the scalps were plentiful, but those who had taken them felt they looked far too nice dangling from their saddles to let them go.

Brown wasn't destined to stay in Fort Stevenson much longer. By the mid-1870s, the American Midwest had changed so much that there was less demand for his skills. The region was no longer the wild expanse it had been a decade earlier. The advancing march of American civilization had pushed the frontier west to Montana. In Dakota, there wasn't much call for guides and interpreters any more, and the military no longer depended on contracted mail carriers. Many Sioux were under the federal government's thumb (though the struggle between Natives and whites continued), and with the buffalo herds an infrequent sight, there were fewer and fewer Natives in the northern area. Violence was giving way to peace.

These developments caused Brown's salary to be reduced by half, from $100 to $50 a month, an amount considerably less than that paid to other civilian employees. Rather than suffer the indignity of working for such a pittance, he quit in disgust. By then his wife Olivia had given birth to a baby girl, and in late summer 1874 Brown moved his small family north to begin a new life with the Métis.

THE CANADIAN WEST
1874-77

HEADING NORTH TO LIVE with Olivia's family couldn't have been a difficult decision for Brown. Likely it followed Olivia's prompting—her people were closely knit and she surely missed them. It's hard to imagine that Brown needed much convincing. In his time with the U.S. Army, he had worked with many Métis. As he became more familiar with their ways, he felt increasingly comfortable around them. They were an optimistic people, easy going and friendly. Brown discovered he had much in common with them, particularly their love for stories and song, and the booze that made both flow so freely. Over the following three years, as Brown hunted and traveled with them in the immense territory bound by the Milk and Saskatchewan rivers, he came to know them intimately. They were a people whose culture was rich, whose free-spirited and determined ways Brown found particularly appealing.

The relatively short, but eventful, history of the Métis greatly influenced the development of these ways. The Métis were among the mixed-blood peoples that emerged during the heyday of the prairie fur trade in the late 18th and 19th centuries. A unique cultural group, the Métis were the off-spring of Native women and European fur traders. The latter were mostly employees of the North West Company, which practiced a distinctly different trading operation than its competitor, the Hudson's Bay Company. Rather than requiring the Natives to bring their furs to the trading post, the North West Company sent its traders, who were for the most part French-speaking laborers, into the frontier to trade with Natives in their territory. Relationships *à la façon du pays*, or according to the customs of the country, soon emerged. Such informal arrangements were of benefit to both parties because the traders—or wintering partners, as they came to be known—depended on Native women to help them survive on the frontier and the Native peoples assured themselves of a regular trading partner. Initially, the children of these relationships were either raised with their mother's people or sent to Montreal (where the North West Company was headquartered) or to Britain for their education.

With the merger of the Hudson's Bay Company and the North West Company in 1821, the old practices of the NWC disappeared and the mixed-blood children, some-times called *bois-brûlés* (or "burnt wood") because of their dark complexion, found themselves increasingly dependent upon the trading posts. Over time, many of them con-cluded that a future subject to the vagaries of trading post life was unappealing, and they decided to break away. They moved east to Red River and west to the plains, and while they occasionally found themselves employed by the fur traders, their main occupation was fur-trade provisioning. Most Métis practiced Roman Catholicism and spoke a mixed French-Cree patois.

The 60 years or so before Brown's arrival had witnessed a number of events that shaped the emergence of the Métis as a distinct people. The Métis were drawn into bloodshed and violence early in the 1800s as the Hudson's Bay Company and the North West Company slugged it out toe-to-toe in an effort to achieve economic supremacy in Rupert's Land. In 1814, when food was in short supply in the HBC stronghold of Red River, Governor Miles Macdonnell issued his "Pemmican Proclamation," which forbade the exportation of pemmican from the district. The intent of the directive was to ensure that there was enough food to nourish the small local community of Scots and former HBC employees. Macdonnell also seized North West Company pemmican supplies, an act designed to disrupt the company's trade. Worse yet, the buffalo hunt was banned because it drove the herds away from the Red River settlers. The proclamation struck at the heart of the Métis economy, and they responded with a campaign of terror over the next year, destroying crops and houses and stealing livestock. Events continued to escalate in the following year, when Cuthbert Grant, the newly chosen Métis leader, and Robert Semple, the colony's newly appointed governor, locked horns.

Grant had concluded that the best way to protect both North West Company and Métis interests was to destroy the Red River colony, an objective clearly reflected in his actions. In the spring of 1816, he captured the Hudson's Bay Company's pemmican brigade, and followed up the aggression with an attack on their local trading post, Brandon House. Having secured the provisions stored at the post, Grant's plan of starving the colonists seemed within reach. As Grant retreated with the supplies, poor traveling conditions unexpectedly forced him to journey close to Red River, where he was spotted by Semple. The governor had been apprised of Grant's attacks, and set out to bring in the men whom he viewed as criminals. Not aware of the size of the Métis contingent, which numbered near 70, Semple quickly organized a party of just over 20 men. They caught up with Grant at Seven Oaks. The two groups held their positions in an uneasy standoff. Grant ordered an aide to convey to Semple the message that he would only accept the governor's surrender. Riding to a point between the two groups, Semple and the Métis messenger stopped. An argument between the two ensued. When Semple grabbed the reins of the Métis' horse, the man abandoned his mount and fled for cover as shots rang out. When the dust settled, Semple and 20 of his men lay dead while only one of Grant's men was slain. Seven Oaks, accident though it may have been, became an important part of Métis history, particularly after it was immortalized by the Métis poet Pierre Falcon, Grant's brother-in-law. The colony was not destroyed, but the Métis had won the right to live according to their customs. There would be no more "Pemmican Proclamations."

The Sayer trial of 1849 further cemented Métis identity. Following the amalgamation of the fur-trading companies, the Hudson's Bay Company, under the headstrong direction of George Simpson, actively sought to protect its trading monopoly. Although the HBC was the only legally recognized trading entity on the prairies of Rupert's Land, an independent trader had established a post beyond the company's reach in Pembina, just south of the American border. The presence of an alternative market for the furs collected in Rupert's Land, limited though it was, proved attractive to many Métis. This competition was a threat to the HBC's hegemony, and the company did all it could to enforce its monopoly. For a number of years in the mid-1840s, Simpson was successful in having British troops posted in the region, ostensibly as protection during the Oregon boundary dispute. The military presence also conveniently

limited illegal trade, but as the crisis fizzled, the troops
departed and the Métis returned to their old practices of
free trade.

The Hudson's Bay Company soon came to realize that
having a monopoly in law and exercising it in fact were not
the same. The HBC decided to take the bull by the horns.
The company brought a Métis named Pierre-Guillaume
Sayer up on charges of illegally trafficking in furs. As the
trial began, the courthouse was surrounded by hundreds of
vocal Métis. The jury found Sayer guilty, but recommended
mercy by pointing out that Sayer had believed his actions
were legal. The judge agreed. Upon emerging from the
courtroom, Sayer was greeted by the roars and celebratory
gunshots of the Métis, who recognized that his freedom
indicated the HBC's impotence in the matter. Without the
force to subdue the military strength of the Métis, and
unable to legally stop the trade, the HBC relented. "Vive la
liberté! La commerce est libre!" the Métis declared; they
had won their battle, thereby removing all threats to the
economic foundation of their way of life.

Events in the early 1850s further demonstrated the
strength of Métis military power. By mid-century, the buffalo hunt, so critical to the Métis way of life, was placed
under increasing stress. No longer was the hunt simply a
matter of a short journey from the Red River. The decimation of the great buffalo herds was well underway, and with
each hunt the Métis were drawn farther west and south in
search of the animals putting them in greater contact with
American Sioux. As Métis hunters depleted their already
dwindling resource, Sioux fury mounted. Worse yet, the
Métis were close relatives of the Cree and Ojibwa, both of
whom were traditional enemies of the Sioux. While hunting, the Métis regularly appointed men as soldiers to be on
the lookout for attacking Sioux, and there were occasional

skirmishes. Matters came to a head in 1851 at the decisive
Battle of Grand Couteau. Though the Métis were outnumbered, their superior military strategy, effectively carried out
with rifles, won the day. On the defensive, the Métis
formed their carts into a circle. Women, children and the
stock took shelter within the makeshift fort. The men
fanned out to a distance of about a gunshot from the carts
and scraped out shallow depressions in the soil. These rifle-
pits offered some limited cover. In the background, an
accompanying priest, waving a crucifix in one hand and a
tomahawk in another, bestowed words of encouragement.
Using their buffalo guns, the Métis inflicted terrible losses
on the Sioux, who soon retreated. The Métis emerged as
the undisputed hunters of the northern prairies.

The benchmark of Métis success in the 19th century
was undoubtedly the Red River Rebellion, which clearly
demonstrated their solidarity and power. The rebellion
rested on the rock-firm pillars of the previous Métis successes, triumphs that gave them the courage to stand
before the nascent Canadian government and declare that
self-determination must direct their political future. The
Métis were driven to armed resistance because of the
nearsighted and insensitive actions of central Canada.
Following Confederation in 1867, Canadian expansionists
began to make real their dream of "settled," agricultural
western territories as the foundation of national prosperity. To maximize economic benefits, settlement was to be
directed by Dominion government officials. Their concern for westerners was minimal, as initially demonstrated
by the purchase of Rupert's Land from the Hudson's Bay
Company in 1869. The vast territory of present-day western and northern Canada included Red River and the
hunting grounds of the Métis. And although the Métis
and the other settlers in Red River had a well-established

The Métis were mixed-blood peoples that emerged during the heyday of the prairie fur trade in the late 18th and 19th centuries. A unique cultural group, the Métis were the offspring of Native women and European fur traders. The latter were mostly employees of the North West Company, which practiced a distinctly different trading operation from its competitor, the Hudson's Bay Company. Rather than requiring the Natives to bring their furs to the trading post, the North West Company sent its traders, who were for the most part French-speaking laborers, into the frontier to trade with the Natives in their territory. Relationships *à la façon du pays* (according to the customs of the country) soon emerged. Such informal arrangements were beneficial to Native groups and traders because the traders depended on Native women to help them survive on the frontier and the Native peoples were assured of regular trading partners and thus a regular supply of European goods.

community, no one from the area was consulted on the sale or on its implications.

Naturally, the turn of events upset the local residents. When a wave of narrow-minded settlers arrived from Ontario and attempted to impose their Anglo-Protestant ways on everyone in ignorance of local traditions, the Métis strongly objected. Resentment boiled over into outright anger when Dominion government land surveyors appeared and imposed a lot system that disrupted long-accepted Métis settlement practices. With the support of much of the non-Métis population, the Métis, under Louis Riel, finally took action. The region declared its independence from Canada. With minimal violence, a delegation from Red River negotiated terms of union with the Dominion government. The result was the creation of the province of Manitoba. While Prime Minister John A. Macdonald limited Métis land rights, effectively restricting their ability to maintain economic viability over the long term, the Métis were initially successful in having their traditional cultural and material practices protected.

When Brown entered the scene in the mid-1870s, Métis culture—which fused elements of Cree, French and Catholic heritages—had reached what might be called its classical stage. The identity of the Red River Métis was firmly established. Comfortably resting on a series of military and political victories, the Métis nation had emerged as a force to be reckoned with. But while these events figured prominently in the development and expression of a Métis identity, they meant little without the buffalo hunt. Upon the great herds of the prairies was founded both a culture and a people.

~~

In the early 1870s, a man perched atop the Cypress Hills in what is now southern Alberta could see a living mass of buffalo merging with the sky on all horizons. Half a decade later, just about all that was left were the wallows, depressions left by bull buffalo as they rolled in the dirt. Brown himself expressed regret about their disappearance, but he recognized it as an inevitable consequence of a changing West. As the great herds of buffalo became a memory, so did much of the culture that they had supported. The traditional Métis way of life that centered on the buffalo hunt fell victim to western transformation.

The relationship between the Métis and the buffalo was an intimate one. Boys became men during the hunt, and girls learned the responsibilities of womanhood. The crooked-backed oxen of the prairies provided for many of the Métis' physical needs. Two- or three-year-old cows were killed for their prime hides. The hides of older cows of five or six years were used for lariats or ropes. They were also valuable in saddle-making. Most of the Métis rode on sewn hides stuffed with antelope hair.

Surprisingly, skinning a dead beast took a skilled worker just a few minutes. The animal was placed *as-thack-a-kay*, on its back, with its head tucked under its shoulders. In winter, when the thicker hide had greater value, skinning was not done close for fear of cutting it. Then, the meat was scraped off with a *mick-a-quaw*, a tool with teeth designed for the purpose. Generally, the hide of a summer buffalo was of little value because of its short hair, and such hides were common enough sights on the prairie grasslands, rotting in the hot sun. The animal's entrails were often found with the abandoned hide, but the Métis used most everything else. The rules of the hunting camp demanded that every part of each animal be used, unless it was diseased. But it was rare for a sick buffalo, usually one with mange or infected through an unhealed wound, to be brought down because ammunition was important enough not to be wasted.

The buffalo were a critical food source, providing some 90 percent of the meat eaten by the Métis. Brown preferred the animal's front quarters because its fattiness was tasty when boiled. The hump and tongue, often pickled in brine, were also eaten. Boiled buffalo calf was considered a delicacy (the Métis never killed young animals, but did bring down pregnant cows). Buffalo marrow made for a flavorful browning sauce. Fresh meat was available only in the few days immediately following the hunt. For the most part the flesh was dried for later consumption, much of it serving as the key ingredient in pemmican.

Either for sale or for sustenance, pemmican was an important product in the Métis economy. To make pemmican, women cut the meat from the flanks and ribs of freshly killed buffalo into thin strips, which were dried and pounded with buffalo fat and berries. There were few on the prairies or in the forested areas to the north who were not, at some time in their lives, sustained by this heavy, nutritious mixture. While the coarse—and if carelessly prepared, hairy—product was definitely an acquired taste, pemmican was ideal for hunters or trappers who were isolated for long periods of time because it never went bad. Brown himself once estimated that, properly prepared, pemmican could last 1000 years.

Native peoples used a variety of strategies to hunt buffalo. If the geography was right, hunters would drive the animals off cliffs. But the more common practice was to direct the animals into pounds or large traps where they could more easily be killed. It was an approach that demanded considerable planning. Piles of branches, called dead men, were placed approximately 15 meters apart to form a converging column. It generally reached a few kilometers from the makeshift pen where the animals were to be driven. Key to the whole operation were the "callers," hunters on horseback who lured the buffalo into the trap. The callers rode out to the herd. Once there, they began to sway back and forth in their saddles and yell. Turning, they rode in a zigzag fashion toward the column's opening. This performance proved magnetic to the buffalo. The animals followed and were funneled through toward the enclosure. Should the buffalo begin to diverge, hunters waving robes leaped from behind the "dead men" and steered the animals in the desired direction. To enter the pen, the buffalo had to jump over a large log about half a meter off the ground. Near the log, inside the enclosure, a depression was dug so that it was impossible for any buffalo to get up enough speed to jump back over the log and escape. Once all the buffalo were inside, the slaughter began.

The Métis were aware of Native hunting practices, but developed a very different hunting tradition that was more to their liking. As with the Native approach, the Métis hunt demanded considerable planning and combined careful organization with unbridled chaos. At the time Brown was a member of the Métis community, all the men voted to elect a chief hunter before the hunt began. This individual was in command of the camp and the hunt; his authority was unquestioned. Advance scouts were dispatched. By the 1870s, the game was often far away and meaningful encounters usually required days of travel before buffalo were close enough to establish camp. Camps were guided by up to 12 men, each with considerable hunting experience. The guide for the day was responsible for raising the camp flag to indicate that it was time to break camp, and for lowering it to show that it was time to stop for the night.

While the flag was raised during travel, the guide of the day assumed authority. The chief hunter once again assumed the role once the flag was lowered.

Decades earlier, in the heyday of great leaders such as Cuthbert Grant and Jean-Baptiste Wilke, the Métis hunt was much larger and the organization of authority was more complex. As many as 10 men were voted as captains, and together they served as the council for the hunt. The senior captain was the chief of the hunt. In addition, each captain had 10 soldiers under his command who acted as a police force and ensured that rules were obeyed. Once the important position of chief hunter had been filled, the whole community would leave their wintering place in search of buffalo. In those days, the hunting community formed lines up to 10 kilometers long.

In Brown's time, a day of travel lasted from early morning until about 6 PM, with only a mid-afternoon break for lunch. Such a schedule allowed the group to cover close to 30 kilometers a day. Generally, the carts used for transportation traveled in columns, with the guide of the day at the front, followed by chief hunter. Slowly they marched, the wooden wheels of the carts squealing against the ungreased wooden axles (grease was ineffective because the dirt it collected served only to gouge and destroy the axles). Some men were assigned soldiering duties to protect the caravan from hostile Sioux.

Once the scouts had found the herd, the Métis struck camp at a distance far enough away to conceal their presence. If the hunt was large enough, the carts were formed into a circle, with the forward shafts of one resting on the tailboard of another. The stock was kept inside the circle, while the tents were set up outside. A broad strategy for the hunt was outlined, but once the kill began it would be every man for himself. Just before most hunts, an accompanying

If ever there was an example of a technology perfectly suited to the needs of those who used it, certainly it was the Métis' Red River cart. It is unclear when the cart first came into use, but it was certainly popular by the early 1800s. The cart was made entirely of wood, held together with leather straps and pulled by either a horse or an ox strapped to two poles extended from the axle. Over the years, the Red River cart was subject to various modifications, but these basic characteristics remained unchanged. The carts were originally rather small, with three-foot solid wheels cut from large trees, and capable of transporting up to 450 pounds. Later, larger wheels with four spokes came into use, and eventually huge, many-spoked wheels appeared, enabling the cart to carry nearly twice as much as it had originally. The large wheels removed most of the challenge of traveling through thick, sticky mud or over hard, baked prairie, and they could easily be removed to allow the cart to float across rivers. Alas, no technology is perfect, and the flaw in the Red River cart was the shrieking of the wheels as they ground against the axles. The wheels could not be greased since lubricants mixed with the dust and dirt thrown up from the trail caused damage to the axle. There was no respite from the ear-jarring noise, which could be heard for long distances.

priest would celebrate mass, praying for a successful hunt, with no men injured. With his portable altar, the priest played an important role in the camp life of the deeply religious Métis. He led in prayers, taught the children catechism, and ministered to the sick and injured. If no priest was present the chief hunter led the camp in prayers.

Muzzle-loaders were the weapons of choice. A hunter held the reins with one hand and used his free hand to take loose gunpowder from his pocket. Throwing it down the barrel, he followed it up with a ball, which he spat from his mouth. With no time for careful packing, the gun stock was struck upon the saddle. The loaded weapon was fired from the waist at a nearby buffalo. To mark his kills, a Métis would throw down a glove or some other personal object. Even without such a marker, the men possessed an uncanny ability to subsequently identify their kills.

Experienced hunters got to within a few meters of their prey before firing. The buffalo runners were quick, able to avoid falling prey and trained to move to the next animal while the rider reloaded. With a fast runner, a good hunter brought down two or three buffalo before most of the men got off a shot. Hit by a misfiring rifle, trampled or gored, men were often injured and sometimes killed. The hunt might last a couple of hours, during which time the best hunters brought down a dozen buffalo, while the less experienced made do with two or three. Perhaps it appeared chaotic, but the skills and grace required rendered it into nothing less than a prairie ballet.

Once the actual hunt was over for the day, the work was not yet done. The men skinned and quartered the carcasses, no pleasant task beneath the relentless glare of the hot prairie sun. It was also long work—even smaller hunts might mean that 1000 buffalo had to be cleaned. The women arrived at the place of slaughter to cart the meat

Métis hunters rode specially trained horses called buffalo runners and they followed the chief hunter as close to the herd as possible without being detected. They then fanned out to the right and left. Within 300 meters the buffalo usually became aware of the hunters' presence and began to move. The chief called "trot," and the men began a slow gallop. When the chief called "equa," they attacked the herd, and the "running of the buffalo" was in full force. For an uninitiated bystander, this process would certainly have appeared chaotic. Stampeding buffalo and swiftly moving horses, cloaked in clouds of dust, danced with a background cacophony of thundering hoofs, bellowing buffalo, shouting Métis and cracking gunfire.

back to camp. Each family was responsible for its own kill, but in times of hardship the chief hunter declared that the buffalo were killed *mini-s-a-wak*, as common property. While the women worked, the men relaxed and discussed the events of the day. Records of who killed how many were made, and if a poor soul embarrassingly admitted to being shut out, he quickly became the butt of jokes. Sputtered excuses fell on deaf ears. The chief hunter also resolved disputes at this time. On the rare occasions that a chief was in doubt as to a decision, a vote was taken. Finally, plans were made for the next day's hunt. By that time, the alcohol was flowing freely.

ᔕᐳᑕ

Caught up in the thrill of the chase, Brown rode his runner along the razor's edge between control and disaster. He was dressed in the colorful garb of the Métis, and his long brown hair flew wildly off his shoulders, matching the horse's mane. His skin was darkened by constant exposure to the sun, and to any observer he might have been one of the Métis with whom he rode. The smells of sweat, dust and gunpowder filled his nostrils, together almost overwhelmed by the sweet, thick odor of blood and the sharp, acrimonious scent of fear. He heard shouts of joy and cries of agony against the thunderous background din of the crazed beasts. He had hunted buffalo before, near the Rockies and down in Montana, but shooting the beasts from a cautious distance did not compare with the thrill of the Métis way of hunting. Absorbing it all, he tried to focus on the task at hand. Even without the challenge of using a muzzle-loader, the hunt tested all his skills. As he fired his Hawkins rifle, Brown caught a glimpse of the fearful and bewildered brown eyes of the animal he brought down. The speed of the hunt gave him little time to reflect on that image because he was already preparing to fire again. It wasn't long before Brown's kill numbered six, a respectable count for any Métis. But he had a fast runner that day and he greedily wanted more.

Brown rode into a new bunch of buffalo and immediately felt the animals begin to crowd in on him. He was a good rider, but his skill was of little value here. The light brush of an occasional beast was replaced by hard bumping and jarring until he lost control of his runner. Kicking wildly, he freed himself from the stirrups and narrowly escaped being dragged through the herd. He found himself looking up at the brownish-yellow dust as it filtered the deep blue sky. This predicament proved little better—the brown fury of stampeding buffalo quickly blocked his sight. Trampled by countless animals, Brown soon lost consciousness, thankfully unaware of the continuing punishment of pounding hooves.

After the buffalo moved on, Brown was finally discovered. A meat cart served as a makeshift ambulance. The bloodied and bruised victim, still unconscious, was unceremoniously transported back to camp. As the cart wheeled up to his tent, Olivia must have been distraught. The sight of her injured husband and the account of his accident did not fill her with confidence about his recovery. Even in a community known for its shared sense of responsibility, a single woman with two children (a second daughter was born while the family lived with the Métis) faced an uncertain and possibly desperate future. She ministered to her man with determination and fortitude. The community joined with her in prayer. Brown responded, his health improved and only a broken shoulder blade took any considerable time to mend. He was laid up for a week and was unable to hunt for the remainder of the season. Still, he gave thanks. Many a hunter was not so lucky after such an experience.

This accident proved to be Brown's closest brush with death during his years with the Métis, but it wasn't his only adventure. As it happened, the event was virtually repeated during his recovery.

One Sunday morning, much of the camp was packed up and ready to move on the following day. The community was celebrating mass with the chief hunter, while Brown was recuperating in his tent. The peaceful interlude was interrupted by a rumbling noise that rapidly intensified. Brown knew that sound. A herd of buffalo was stampeding toward the camp!

Brown grabbed his rifle and leaped from the tent, his pain tamped down by his resolve. He saw that the animals were no longer in the distance—they were little more than a stone's throw away. The herd's size was impossible to gauge in all the dust, but Brown could tell from the noise that it was large. The moving body showed no signs of stopping, or of veering off in another direction. Fleetingly, Brown wondered why a herd would be on a crash course for the encampment, but the thought was quickly lost in the urgency of the situation. Swift action was required, even though Brown realized that the efforts of any one man, even a healthy one, could only be futile.

He rested the barrel of his rifle on a cart and fired a couple of shots. They had all the impact of an irritating blackfly on the stampeding herd. The animals broke into the camp as if it were nothing more than a continuing stretch of open prairie. Unable to stop the charge, Brown must have stood awestruck by the simple power of the beasts. They upset tents, reducing many to tatters. They overturned carts as easily as one flipped a pancake, destroying wheels and shafts in the process. Like a prairie thunderstorm, the stampede

was over almost as soon as it had begun. All that remained
of the herd's presence was a swath of destruction through
the center of the camp. Had the Métis not been at mass, the
human toll would have been staggering.

Once the herd had departed, the cause of the stampede
became apparent. Following the buffalo was a party of
white hunters who had apparently spooked the animals
into flight. When the men saw the destruction they had
unwittingly caused, they vamoosed at full gallop.

Aside from such mishaps, Brown was comfortable living
with the people of the plains. The transient Métis camp life
proved magnetic to Brown, allowing him to scratch his itchy
feet. He was no less impressed with the thoughtfulness that
the Métis put into the location and construction of their
winter camps, which were generally used from late
November to May. Many factors influenced their settlement
decisions, but access to wood, water and buffalo was critical.
Their cabin design proved quite influential on Brown; he
later modeled his Kootenay home on the Métis style.

The greatest attraction for Brown was the Métis tem-
perament. They were a joyful people, given to having a
good time and enjoying life. In the winter camp, dancing
was a nightly affair. Fiddles played Red River jigs and feet
moved in harmony with the bow as light from the fire
threw distorted shadows on the walls. The music and dancing were close cousins to forms of Celtic recreation, and
they surely brought back memories of Brown's Irish childhood. Often, such dances were private affairs, in which a
neighbor invited a few friends. However, some winter
camps boasted larger dance halls where Métis from nearby
communities came and shared in the revelry. These were no
small events. Brown lived in a community of about 1000
residents, and few chose not to celebrate when presented
with the opportunity. Language proved no barrier because

During summer the Métis lived in tents while they hunted buffalo, but in other seasons their lodgings were more substantial wooden dwellings, as seen here. The houses could accommodate, on average, seven people. Peeled logs formed the cabin walls and, when split, formed the floor as well. The oversized fireplaces were connected to chimneys made of rocks and plastered mud. Their cavernous openings provided all the illumination that was necessary, so lights of any other sort were rare. Two-meter logs were swiftly devoured in the fireplaces, easily shooting flames three meters into the air. From a distance, the nighttime vista of a Métis camp appeared as so many candles flickering in the moonlight.

Brown, who already spoke French and Cree, experienced little difficulty learning the local patois.

But there were challenges, insignificant as they might have been, and Brown's actions occasionally marked him as different from the community as a whole. For example, he did not share the Catholicism of the Métis, although their faith influenced him nonetheless. By this time, it appears that Brown was no longer a Christian and had already embarked on his own divergent spiritual journey. Brown never met a more deeply religious people than the Métis, and the sincerity of their devotion gave him pause to more fully consider his own. Likely, this pause was a key step on his road to embracing Theosophy some years later. While with the Métis, however, his not being a Catholic set into motion a series of events that was to land him in some trouble.

Camp rules dictated that all members attend mass on Sunday, but for some reason lost to history on this occasion Brown, who usually attended service with Olivia, had shirked that duty. Alone in sin, Brown sighted an antelope. This posed a significant problem. To see such a creature was rare enough, but to have one wander so close to camp was unheard of. Its fresh meat would be a pleasing change from pemmican. However, there was a standing camp rule that no rifle was to be fired on a Sunday; the Métis took seriously the commandment that the Lord's Day was one of rest. Brown was aware of the hefty fine for breaking this rule, but the temptation proved overwhelming. Taking his rifle, he advanced on the antelope and, when close enough, he brought it down. The celebrants at mass heard the shot and two *sa-mag-inis-uck* were quickly dispatched to arrest the transgressor. The following day, Brown appeared before the chief hunter.

"Brown," the chief hunter began, "you live among us because of your relationship wit' the Lyonnais woman, not because you are Métis. Still, we accept you as one of us, and as a member of our community, you must live by the rules set by all, for all."

Brown nodded and remained silent.

"You are aware that the crack of the rifle is not to be 'eard on the day of the Lord?" the chief hunter asked.

Again Brown nodded.

"And yet you fired?"

"Yes. But…but, I shot an antelope—fresh meat," Brown replied in a feeble attempt to defend himself.

"On Sunday, we rest as God did. We respect 'im by laying down our rifles. For the sacrifice of 'is Son, we can do wit'out fresh meat. You will pay a $10 fine."

Suitably rebuked, Brown left the chief and set out to make good on his fine. Because there was never money in a Métis camp, Brown fulfilled his punishment by paying an equivalent amount in meat. And, save for his experience with the stampeding buffalo, which was either forgiven or unknown, he never again broke this rule. There is no record as to whether he got to eat the meat of the antelope.

ॐ

By the late 1870s, a man could travel from the Milk River to the Saskatchewan River and not see a single buffalo. While the decimation of the great herds had devastating consequences for the Métis way of life, for Brown it simply meant that it was time to pull up stakes and find a new way to make a living. Change was nothing new to him and, on this occasion, it was probably eased by leaving behind the increasingly chafing restraints of life in the Métis community. However, his situation was somewhat different than it had been previously. Brown left his family with their Métis relatives and turned to wolfing. It was an occupation offering easy money, quickly.

Wolf hunters were in great demand because of the damage the animals did to livestock of the newly emerging ranching business. Wolves killed more cattle on the prairies than all other predatory animals combined. Their attacks were vicious. Hunting in packs, they separated an animal from the herd. Mostly, they attacked calves and cows, but a full-grown bull could easily be a victim if they were hungry enough. The vicious wolves proved enough of a problem to the ranchers that they were willing to pay $2.50 per hide. This incentive was enough to make wolfing an attractive occupation because expenses were low. Brown and his partners made $2500 one winter and their only real cash outlay was for strychnine. When supplies of the poison were short, wolfers might be charged up to $8 for a small bottle, but the price was generally around $5 or $6.

Wolfing was hardly labor intensive—the only physical exertion required was to prepare the bait and skin the dead wolf—but it did require some skill. Wolfers often used buffalo as bait. After shooting one of the beasts, they lay the carcass on its back, spread-eagle. The legs were skinned on the inside and the abdomen was cut open to the ground. The heart, liver and some of the other organs were removed, cut into small pieces and placed in a tub. There they were liberally doused with strychnine. These pieces were then rubbed all over the carcass, with particular care given to the meat left in strips on the ribs. Differing amounts of strychnine were required depending on the size of the buffalo. A full-grown bull required four bottles; a two-year-old animal required two; and a calf needed only a bottle.

Once the carcass had been poisoned, the wolfers had to keep the wolves away from the bait until it had time to freeze. If the meat was fresh, a few wolves could easily eat all the bait and thereby waste it, because just a quarter of a kilogram or so of poisoned meat was enough to kill a wolf. When the bait was frozen, the wolves were unable to eat as quickly or as much. It is also possible that the frozen meat took the bitter edge off the taste of the strychnine, a taste that sometimes proved strong enough for wolves to reject the free meal. The desirability of freezing the meat meant that most wolfing was done in the cold months. The morning after a trap was set, Brown usually found about 20 dead wolves, although as many as 50 or 60 scattered carcasses were not uncommon. One of Brown's partners told him of a big bull that had been the final meal for 125 wolves. When death came to the wolves, it must have been a relief for them—the poisoning was slow and painful.

The wolfers were a rough lot, considered by many to be the lowest form of human life on the prairies. The common use of strychnine saddled them with a particularly bad reputation. The key problem was that wolves were not the only animals to eat the bait. It was irresistible to the dogs owned by Natives, and it occasionally even poisoned a hungry Native or two. Wolves were also sacred animals to many Natives, and to see the animals destroyed so carelessly and so cruelly raised their ire. Perhaps even more than the whisky traders who demoralized them with firewater and the hide hunters who decimated the buffalo herds, the wolfers were despised by the Natives. Disputes between wolfers and Natives became increasingly common, and bloodshed became the norm.

A few years before Brown became an active wolfer, in fact, tensions between wolfers and Natives broke with great force near the Cypress Hills, where the wolfers' violent nature collided with the frustration and resentment of the local Assiniboines. As rifles met bows, the outcome was predictable.

The Green River Renegades were a group of wolfers, mostly American, but with a few Canadians, out of Fort Benton, Montana. One fateful day, they discovered that about 40 of their horses had been stolen. In true vigilante fashion, they rode north into Canada to the whisky post of Fort Farwell. There the trail went cold. Over more than a few bottles of booze, they discussed their next move. The choice became clear after a few terse words from a fellow patron.

"Stinkin' redskins," he exclaimed. "I jus' had t' give one a bottle of whisky t' get back m' horse. Claims he foun' it, but I'm sure he was the one who stole it in the firs' place. Damn horse thieves, every one of them."

His comments raised the suspicions of the vigilantes and made up their drunken minds that they were on the right trail.

Abel Farwell, the proprietor of the establishment, tried to make reason prevail. "There's no way that these Assiniboines stole your horses," Farwell said. "They've been camped near here for the winter. No way they coulda got down to Benton. Ain't got many horses anyhow."

The vigilantes ignored Farwell and rode out to the Assiniboines' camp. Arriving drunk, they were met by Natives who shared their condition.

"Where's our horses?" the leader asked.

"No horses," came the reply.

Fuelled by alcohol, questions and answers transformed into bullets and arrows. When the dust settled, one wolfer lay dead, while some 30 Assiniboines had been cut down by high-powered rifles. An elder was further brutalized when the men decapitated him. Impaling the bloody head on a sharpened stick, they brought it back to Fort Farwell and left it at the gate as a reminder to all Natives not to mess with wolfers.

It wasn't easy to escape a violent reputation with such activities as these. Nothing suggests that Brown participated in such violence. By the time he became involved in wolfing, he had considerable experience, both good and bad, in dealing with Natives. It was true that Brown had an explosive temper, but it was launched only on occasion, and usually with good cause. Much more commonly expressed was his good nature and humor, as is evident in the way he and his partners helped some wolfing novices.

Brown was sitting around the campfire with his fellow wolfers. They typically hunted in small parties of up to 10 men; there were six wolfers in this group. They were making plans for the next day's hunt when a couple of newcomers, or *cheechako*, rode into camp. From their stiffness in the saddles to their new clothes, everything about them marked the duo as new to the trade. Brown asked them to sit a spell, and while enjoying a mug of coffee, they soon shared their reason for dropping by.

"Boys, we're new to these parts," one of them explained. "We heard there was barrels of easy money to be made wolf hunting. But we just can't seem to get this strychnine business down. The best we can figure is that we're not using the poison right. The wolves are eating the bait and just getting fatter." He raised a pint bottle of the deadly liquid in one hand. "We were hoping that you might be able to give us some advice."

"Why don't you let us take a closer look at that," said Bill Martin, a long-time wolfer.

The bottle was uncorked and passed among the men, each of whom took a deep whiff. When the bottle finally reached old Bill, he asked if he could taste it. With a puzzled look, the tenderfoot gave his consent. Martin retrieved a spoon and swallowed a healthy dose of the liquid, whereupon he started to cough.

"Boys, I've had enough of this life," he began, between ragged breaths. "Brown, you take my old Pinto mare. She ain't much, but she'll get you where you need to go. Preston, make good use of my Hawkins rifle." With that, Martin walked over to his bedroll and lay down.

The shocked *cheechako* implored Brown and his companions to help the dying man, but no one would move. In desperation, one of them grabbed a pot of wolf grease, which made for a flavorful sauce, and tried to force it down old Bill's throat.

"Leave me be," he moaned. "I'm tired, and I want to die."

After some time, it became apparent that Martin was not going to die. While it was unknown to the *cheechako*, the wolfers were all aware that the bottle didn't contain strychnine. The smell was all wrong and the poison never came in pint bottles. Turns out that the two men had been swindled into buying a mixture of Epsom salts and saltpeter. Old Bill was a little sick, but it was nothing that a respectable shot of whisky couldn't cure, and a bellyache was a cheap price to pay for the laughs enjoyed. The newcomers joined Brown's bunch, and by spring they had become pretty good at the job.

Although wolfing provided a good income, Brown would have thrown away every penny to avoid what lay ahead. The largest market for the hides was in Fort Benton, and in an effort to get the best return he could on his winter work, Brown headed for the Montana trading hub in the spring of 1877. There, unforeseen events were to bring him far too close to the hangman's noose.

"KOOTENAI"
1877-90

DYING WAS EASY in Fort Benton. It was the type of place where arguments were settled with smoking iron and bloodied steel, where the man left standing was the one with the best case. John Brown found himself a party in just such a dispute. While he always had a way with words, the exclamation point to this case was a knife in the gut of one Louis Ell. Whether Ell saw the truth of Brown's position before his last breath will forever remain a mystery. For Brown's part, his brush with American justice was to leave him a changed man, content in the welcoming arms of nature and the comforting restraints of British law north of the 49th parallel.

The history of Fort Benton was short and rough, stretching back only as far as the mid-19th century. Located in upper Montana, it was ideally situated at the northern reaches of the Missouri River. Ready access to that great river meant that markets to the south easily supplied the fort and points beyond. Initially, the fort served as a trading post for the American Fur Company. Its steamers plied the

Missouri, arriving with trade goods and other necessities and leaving with great bales of buffalo hides and wolf skins. By the late 1860s, the fort was leased to the United States government and was used as a military post. With the stability provided by the army's presence, Fort Benton came to be a popular supply post for the many small communities scattered around it on both sides of the international border.

As a result of its function as a service center, the popular cliché was that all trails led out of Fort Benton—the "Chicago of the plains." Common sights on those trails were wagons, mule trains and bull trains, each of which regularly fanned out from the town. The mule trains were built for speed, though speed was a relative concept on the rutted and often muddied northern trails. With up to eight pairs of mules, an experienced skinner could make the run to Fort Macleod, for example, in a week and a half. And the cargo that had to move so fast? Whisky and guns. With such attractive supplies, a mule-train outfit could clean out a Native's supply of winter furs while a bull train lumbered along, days behind.

In the 1860s, there was about as much civilization in Fort Benton as there was water in the good whisky that the smuggler kept for himself. It was a place given a wide berth by the handful of easterners who traveled in the northwest. While the town served as a military and supply post, its economy had other important supports, including trade with Native peoples, whisky smuggling and gold mining. None of these operations was conducive to refined manners and eastern social mores, and without the critical civilizing presence of religion, the place glowed raw red.

The town was in the heart of Blackfoot country, and the Blackfoot presence was an unsettling one. Through most of the 1860s, the Blackfoot War raged and the Natives' warpainted faces unmistakably marked their hostility.

The bull trains were large operations, consisting of eight to ten pair of oxen pulling up to three wagons and, when so organized, the outfit could easily stretch out for almost a mile. They carried a good selection of cargo, including food and other frontier supplies. A bull train's team included a train boss, a night herder and a boy who did odd jobs. But the key member was the bullwhacker. He controlled the animals, ensuring a steady gait with a well-placed crack of a bullwhip—a meter of rawhide extending from a two-meter handle. Expertly used, the bullwhip raised a welt the size of a prize-winning cucumber on a beast's flank, while the bullwhacker's colorful language raised the small hairs on a man's neck anywhere within a five-kilometer radius. Bull trains lumbered along slowly, at best covering about 20 kilometers a day, making the journey to Fort Macleod a three-week affair. Slow they might have been, but for the merchants and residents of Fort Benton, the clouds of dust stirred up by these outfits had all the glitter of gold.

Blackfoot anger was not dulled by the unscrupulous activities of the whisky traders, whose swill contributed to more
than one violent outburst. Not all the Natives were out for
bear, though. Friendly Peigan were so common in town
that they might as well have been residents. They were also
victims of booze and, increasingly, of poverty. The military
presence was designed to deal with this situation, but their
own track record of bloodshed was hardly inspirational.
More often than not, the army's policy was to maintain
firm control, by whatever means possible. And military folks
were far from saints. They enjoyed a whoop-up as much as
any of the other residents.

Smugglers like Sweet-Oil Bob or Whisky Dick made up
a good portion of the town's community. These folks were
not given to calm consideration and discussion of disagreements; too many words were a burden on the tongue. Hard
men, they were as ready to whip out a revolver as they were
to throw back a shot of booze, and they were unlikely to
reflect on the moral merits of either act. If, on a dark night,
a fellow was to encounter Liver-Eating Johnson, who came
by his name in a straightforward and bloody fashion, that
fellow might not be too concerned about the morality of
being the first to draw a gun, either. If he waited for local
law enforcement to show up and help, well, it's likely that
his liver would have long since been served up by the time
such help arrived.

Besides, odds were excellent that the sheriff was as
crooked as the criminal. It wasn't unknown for a sheriff to
use his inside knowledge of successful bull- or mule-train
outfits, or miners who had struck it rich, to pick such folks
clean once they were out of town. One man with a star
even took to lightening the purses of drunkards who found
themselves spending the night in his cell—an expensive
room, indeed! If the sheriff didn't trade in whisky, he was

Construction on Fort Benton from the remnants of Fort Lewis down-stream began in the spring of 1846. It was the last fur-trading post on the Upper Missouri and marked the beginning of the Whoop-Up Trail on which traders freighted goods and carried on an illicit trade in whisky from Fort Benton to Fort Whoop-Up in what is now southern Alberta. In 1848, the fort was rebuilt with adobe bricks made from Upper Missouri clay, because it was thought that adobe would provide better protection against the harsh northern winters. The fort itself was built in a 150-foot square quadrangle and enclosed buildings such as the trade store, warehouse, kitchen, blacksmith, carpenter, barn and housing quarters for agents and their employees. When the fur and robe trade came to an end, the American Fur Company sold the fort to the military who abandoned it in 1875. By the time John Brown came on the scene in the late 1870s, Fort Benton wasn't the raw fron-tier town it had been a decade earlier. By and large, the old economy had given way to one based on the commercial interests of financiers, freighters and wholesalers.

likely paid off by those who did. And just about everybody did. Even the town's most prominent citizens, merchant-house proprietors like T.C. Power and I.G. Baker, were deeply involved. Deny it they might, but the sale of booze added significantly to their bottom lines and kept the Whoop-Up country nice and wet.

With the news of the gold strike at nearby Last Chance Gulch in the mid-1860s, thousands of lusty and wild-eyed miners turned Fort Benton into a boomtown. Those lured by prospects of gold were not ones inclined to be model citizens. Often they were as much running *from* civilized life as they were running *to* the gold fields. Accompanying this motley assortment of residents were all the trappings of a crude frontier town—saloons, gambling and prostitution.

By the late 1870s, Fort Benton wasn't the raw frontier town it had been a decade earlier. By and large, the old economy had given way to one based on the commercial interests of financiers, freighters and wholesalers. As respectable businessmen sought to protect their interests, stability and order became important. But the attitudes that characterized the old practices didn't fade away quite so quickly. More than one "respectable" town booster had been a smuggler in a past life. As for the town's recreations, they were still there—perhaps just little less visible, but hardly less enjoyed. Trouble was still all too easy to find in Fort Benton.

ᔕᓬᔓ

Trouble came looking for John Brown. It wasn't as if he was hiding from it, though. Indeed, his raging temper tended to make trouble inevitable. Since leaving the Métis, Brown had derived a significant portion of his income from trading goods at Fort Benton. The spring thaw found him and his family journeying to the southern post, where he traded the wolf skins and other furs he had taken over the winter. Fort Benton was always a nasty place, and it possessed an even sharper edge in the spring, when many men like Brown congregated there to do business. The fort's temporary residents were not the most sociable of folks, and local residents often appeared as monuments of propriety by comparison. The stress of living in a confined area with so many other people was disorienting for those used to the solitary life of the trapper, and tempers flared. Angry words were readily followed by violent physical eruptions. Brown, knowing something of his own nature by this time, sought to avoid the town as much as possible. He chose to make his camp near the fort with his wife and her Métis relatives. Despite his precautions, the spring of 1877 proved unique. Brown was arrested as he fled north on the Whoop-Up Trail. The charge was murder.

The details of the murder have been mostly lost in the sketchy yellow journalism so characteristic of the time. When the case was first reported in the newspapers, it was said that Brown had viciously, and with premeditation, attacked a Frenchman named Louis Ell. According to these news stories, the incident was related to a debt the victim had incurred and passed on to Brown. Unwilling to vouch for Ell, Brown, according to these highly sensationalized accounts, used a butcher knife to rip open the man's stomach. The vicious slash was said to have split the victim in two pieces, leaving him dead before either part hit the ground.

While Brown certainly had the temper to commit such a grisly act, the account that subsequently emerged from an eyewitness cast a new light on the incident.

According to the eyewitness, Brown and Ell were arguing, the harsh words of one drowning out those of the other.

"You're a damn liar," one of them shouted.

Apparently, that was enough talk. Somehow Brown plunged his knife into Ell's chest. As Brown pulled the bloody knife from the wound, a Métis who had heard the quarrelling broke onto the scene. Ell stumbled toward this newcomer, desperately seeking protection. Brown was quick on Ell's heels, but the Métis interfered with his continued attack.

"Mister, you'd best mind your own business if you don't want some of the same," snarled Brown.

The Métis retreated into his tent. Brown took a step toward Ell, who lay prostrate on the ground, blood seeping from between the fingers that desperately sought to plug the wound. Before Brown could make certain of Ell's death, the Métis reappeared brandishing a knife of his own. His blood boiling and his reason evaporated, Brown made a beeline for the man. The two men met at the door of the tent and grabbed each other. They wrestled and tumbled to the ground, where Brown dropped his knife. The Métis retrieved it, and Brown ran for his horse and fled the scene. Minutes later, Ell died.

Brown beat a hasty retreat north, for the most part steering clear of the well-traveled routes. He was alone, his family unaware of the recent event. But they would be safe enough with their Métis relatives, at least for the time being. As Brown rode, he must have reflected on the seriousness of his situation. American justice on the frontier was swift and deadly, and consideration of the facts was sometimes an unwelcome and easily avoided obstacle on the short trip to the nearest dead-man's tree. Brown knew of Ell's local popularity and figured the trader had plenty of contacts who would likely seek revenge, either through vigilante action or by applying pressure on the court system. The 49th parallel was his salvation, and he made for it with a single-minded determination. As he rode hard, Brown finally understood why the Natives called the boundary the Medicine Line. The line was invisible, but it would stop any pursuing American lawmen dead in their tracks. If Brown crossed it, he'd be free—and that *was* good medicine. Unfortunately, Sheriff Rowe, a veteran of the Whoop-Up days, tracked him down. The man knew the ins and outs of the northern territory like a wolf knows its home range. Whether Brown surrendered or put up a fight has been lost to history. His hands shackled, his eyes lifeless, the prisoner was taken to the Fort Benton jail.

From the first, Brown pleaded self-defense, but those words fell like rain on a well-oiled duster. The sheriff had heard it all before. And the townsfolk weren't interested in Brown's possible innocence; they were out to prove that Fort Benton was a town of peace and justice, where an honest man could do business. A no-nonsense hanging was a sure-fire way to underline that message. But Brown was never one to dance to another's tune; fearful that only a short future awaited him, he took matters into his own hands.

After spending several weeks in jail, Brown attempted suicide. He stabbed himself in the chest with a small makeshift knife provided by a fellow inmate. The observant new sheriff, John Healy, foiled the suicide. As he entered the cell with Brown's breakfast, his suspicions were piqued when he found the inmate wearing an overcoat. Healy watched as Brown paced the cell in an erratic fashion with his hand pressed to his chest. Finally the sheriff drew his revolver and ordered Brown to raise his hands. As Brown followed instructions, both the knife, still clutched in one hand, and the seeping wound in his chest were revealed. Medical assistance was summoned, and the doctor treated what was identified as nothing more than a minor wound.

In the doctor's considered opinion, Brown was insane. His depression was such that he may well have been mentally ill. Brown was placed under regular supervision.

In the fall Brown was taken to the territorial capital of Helena to stand trial. He must have been relieved that he hadn't met his end at the hands of a pack of vigilantes. Even so, as he set out on the road south, he had new troubles. It was all too likely that the court would now finish the job he had started some months back. The trip itself proved uneventful, and Brown soon found himself being judged under the stars and stripes.

"How does the prisoner plead?" asked the judge.

"Not guilty," Brown replied. He sat motionless in the prisoner's dock, the terror of the situation overwhelming. For the first time in his life, he found himself in a position where he could do nothing. Sure, he could make his case, and be persuasive at it, but the outcome rested in the deliberations of 12 strangers. For a man used to following his own star and depending on the efforts of none but himself, the situation was unbearable.

The trial lasted two days and, as Brown listened, there was little in the evidence that seemed in his favor. In particular, Sheriff Healy painted Brown as an evil man, while Ell was described in such glowing terms that even Brown must have reconsidered whether he had done the world a disservice in effecting the man's early exit.

But Sheriff John Healy's reputation seems to have preceded him. Few didn't know that he was the rajah of rotgut, the big man of the Whoop-Up whisky trade. And he was given to swagger and bombast, characteristics that might well have undermined his testimony. The jurors were anything but naive and were aware that words could mask the truth of an event as easily as they could reveal it. And they knew that on the frontier a man sometimes had to provide his own justice.

Apparently they agreed that this was exactly what Brown had done, because they returned a verdict of not guilty. While Brown rarely spoke of this event in later years, he did tell a friend that those two words were the most wonderful in the English language.

The words "not guilty" must have echoed through his mind and liberated his soul as Brown rode north. The reunion with his family near Fort Benton was as worthy an occasion for celebration as he was likely to see. Somber goodbyes had long since been expressed because most expected that Brown would see the harsher side of frontier justice. Back-slapping "yee-haw" welcomes greeted his return. Brown always enjoyed a party and he surely was of a mind to celebrate, but he had no inclination to do it in the United States.

As soon as possible, Brown loaded up his family and they made their way to Canada by wagon along the Whoop-Up Trail. Only when he crossed the 49th parallel did Brown feel secure. He put his Benton experience behind him and it only resurfaced in the occasional nightmare. Brown took his family to the Kootenay Lakes, a place he had long ago identified as the spot he wanted to call home, and dropped anchor. His wandering days were over. In the years that followed, John Brown became "Kootenai" Brown, a legendary figure in the region and a colorful member of the community.

ᔕᔕ

Brown soon teamed up with Fred Kanouse, a businessman operating out of Fort Macleod. Kanouse was a onetime Montana sheriff who had fled north after killing a man in an argument over a horse. Flight into the Canadian

Whoop-Up country allowed him to participate fully in the whisky trade; as a sheriff, he had been more of a part-timer. He was later one of the original settlers in the Fort Macleod region and was the first man to import cattle into the foothills.

Kanouse owned a small cabin on the eastern shore of Upper Kootenay Lake, where he grazed his herd and traded with local Natives. In late 1877, Brown moved into the cabin, using it as both a store and a homestead. It was a decent enough business; Brown and Kanouse possessed thousands of dollars worth of stock, shipped from Benton by way of Macleod. The cabin soon became a busy place. Kootenay, Nez Perce and Flathead wandered in to trade, and what languages Brown didn't know, he mastered soon enough. The trading post might have been even more profitable had Brown chosen to liquor up the Natives, but he had long since learned that Natives and whisky didn't mix. Despite Native demands for alcohol, Brown traded very little booze.

The cabin also served as a gaming house after Brown discovered that the Natives loved to gamble. It was a happy match, as Brown was also fond of games of chance. Many an hour was whiled away in a variety of gambling recreations. The Kootenay and Flathead were drawn to card games, and they were pretty good at it. Cards weren't Brown's forte, so Kanouse played all the poker. Brown's interest lay in shooting and racing, both on foot and on horseback. Brown and Kanouse came to see games of chance as part of their business, the winnings serving up a handsome percentage of their profits. Their regular gambling earnings didn't sit well with the Natives, who almost invariably found their hard-earned trade goods sorely depleted. Angry Natives were dangerous ones, and Brown was regularly forced to rectify their losses or face serious trouble. Sometimes this meant adding a "tail"—gifts given before a trading party departed—to the deal. The tail was designed to mollify Native anger, which invariably surfaced when the Natives discovered that they had received too little in return for their furs. Mostly, the poor trading was attributable to alcohol, but the tail was used whenever there were hard feelings that a white trader wanted to avoid. Other times required more creative solutions.

Brown and Kanouse kept a couple of horses that they used only for racing. Honest John handled the long distances and Sleepy ran the quarter-mile. Try as they might to find a champion, the Natives' horses could never best these two. Defeat, however, proved to be no deterrent.

On one occasion a band of Kootenay were in to trade. They brought in some quality furs and had bartered for some $500 worth of goods. When the dealing was done, one of the braves spoke. "We want to race. We have a new cayuse. Good runner."

"Well, you boys know that I'm always up for a race," smiled Brown. "But you don't have any furs left, and we know you don't have any money. So what are we going to use for stakes?"

The braves turned to their packhorses. They unloaded everything they had just bought. Soon piled in front of the store door was a hodgepodge of saddles, bridles, blankets, cloth…all brand, spanking new. To boot, the Kootenay rounded up 40 cayuses they had with them. Brown figured they were worth about $20 each.

"Where is your stake?" asked one of the braves.

Kanouse went into the store and brought back $500 in cash. It didn't nearly match the Natives' stake, but no one paid that any mind. The braves nodded in agreement and grunted their acceptance. With that, the race was on, but it wasn't much of a contest. Honest John was already enjoying a celebratory rubdown when the Kootenay horse crossed the finish line.

The braves took the loss in stride; easy come, easy go was their philosophy. The women with them, however, saw matters in a different light.

"You men are fools. No, you are sons of fools. Foolishness runs in your blood like water through the riverbed," they chided. "These white men have tricked you. Winter comes, and now we have no warm clothes or furs to trade. We will not keep you warm," they threatened.

The situation was starting to turn ugly. Brown looked around. There were some 70 braves, but he, Kanouse and Charlie Miller were the only whites. Things could get plenty uglier—and fast.

"We better give these redskins something," Kanouse mumbled to Brown. "Damn sure there's going to be trouble if we don't."

Brown nodded. He walked over to the braves.

"My brothers, trade's been good for us this year," Brown said. "We want to share with our good friends, the Kootenay. We have one blanket for every squaw and a knife or plug of tobacco for every brave. And we don't want our friends to walk home. That is not fit for warriors. We also give you 20 of the cayuses."

The braves nodded; their women fell silent. They soon left, evidently content. Brown and Kanouse felt pretty good. After all, they had kept the best horses for themselves.

In spite of these early successes, it wasn't long before business went bad. The Natives who had once traveled up from the United States began to trade on the south side of the border. Brown sold out his trading interest to Kanouse, who continued the business for another year.

Without a place to live, Brown built a new log cabin farther along the lakeshore. He was able to make a good life for his family. Game and fish were plentiful. As a hunter and fisherman, Brown again found himself trading, though he was a seller and not a buyer. Such activities increasingly found him in Fort Macleod. While there, his reputation grew in leaps and bounds. His comments on the Kootenay Lakes were frequently printed in the local paper. Newspaper reports similar to this one also made it known that he was available to guide parties into the region:

Spring has arrived in Macleod, and so has Kootenai Brown. He reports that there is no shortage of wildlife in the region and the quality and number of furs he has brought in to trade are a testament to that. His knowledge of the mountain terrain and passes and of the wildlife habitat make him an excellent choice for your hunting guide. Brown also has in his possession a 30-pound lake trout. While readers are rightly wise to the stink of fishy tales, this reporter can vouch for the veracity of this catch. Brown has a boat on the upper lake, and can provide all necessary tackle, whether one wants to troll or fly-fish. If you want to return from your fishing trip with more than a tall tale, see Kootenai Brown, for he catches fish where others fail.

In promoting his services, Brown was also busy publicizing the bounty and beauty of the region. His celebrity as a guide coincided with the beginning of the region's popularity among those who enjoyed the variety of outdoor recreations it had to offer. Once Brown started, he never stopped spreading the good news of the Kootenay Lakes. His actions were the first steps along the path of protection. Once strangers saw the place, reports of its majesty became commonplace and pressures mounted for government action to ensure that the place remain pristine.

∽∾

Kootenai Brown's solid and colorful reputation translated into steady employment as a guide. Clients sought him out so that they might benefit from both his expertise and his stories of the early days. Brown wasn't picky. He guided the rich, the powerful and the ordinary people who were simply seeking adventure or the prospect of bringing down some big game. Among his clients were the Earl of Lathom, the Canadian Minister of Customs Mackenzie Bowell, and countless scores of others whose personages were deemed unworthy to be recorded by history.

The Earl of Lathom, an Englishman, was a rancher in southern Alberta and, along with A.S. Hill, a Member of Parliament in Britain, an owner of the Oxley Ranch Company. These men, like a handful of other wealthy entrepreneurs, took advantage of a Dominion government policy that allowed for the long-term lease of enormous chunks of prairie land at low costs. Lathom was a perfect representative of the ranching community's upper echelon, which was mostly British and upper class. Other owners couldn't always boast his blue blood, but they could easily trace roots back to the old country. The tendency toward high culture set by the owners was reinforced by the many remittance men who soon populated the area. Generally the younger sons of British nobility who faced poor prospects of succession, they were packed off to the colonies with a stipend regularly remitted by their families. There was an unmistakably British mark stamped on the early years of European settlement in the ranching country, which existed in relatively easy harmony with the American culture brought from the south by the cowboys who worked the cattle.

Faced with carving a living from nature, the first ranchers endured the primitive conditions encountered by all

immigrants to the West. By the 1880s, they had achieved a
respectable level of comfort. Log houses replaced the tents
and, in turn, log houses gave way to frame houses with
internal decors that were decidedly Victorian. Personal ser-
vants took care of the needs of the master and mistress.
Fashions were a reflection, though often imperfect, of
London trends. Sports and pastimes more accurately mirrored the activities of memory, and, because ranch ownership proved less than labor intensive, there was plenty of
leisure time to allow for indulgence. Cricket, polo and ten-
nis were popular among the ranching community and they
shared these recreational tastes with the Mounties and
other residents of Fort Macleod. The ladies likely found
the many gala balls more to their tastes, and they ensured
that the events were true, in both costume and dance, to
the accepted British norm. Intellectual life did not suffer,
either. Ranchers were well-educated people, and both the
cultural climate and leisure opportunities were ones that
allowed for, and respected, those whose tastes turned in
that direction.

Brown spent a fair amount of time at the homes of the
ranchers in his vicinity, particularly the adjacent Cochrane
spread. Although Brown was Irish, his Anglican upbringing,
good education and military service ensured a certain
degree of comfort and acceptance in the ranchers' cultural
milieu. In September 1883, Brown was contracted by
Lathom, Hill and some of the other owners of the Oxley to
act as a guide on a hunting and fishing trip into the
Kootenay Lakes area. Having heard about Brown and his
British roots, the group was somewhat surprised when they
reached his cabin and found a wild-looking, long-haired
man in a slouch hat, strange garments and moccasins, a man
for whom any European heritage appeared but a distant
memory.

"Dear God," muttered one of the party. "You're certain the man's British?"

"Irish, at least," came the reply.

"Ahhh, yes, that explains it."

Still, Brown's reputation preceded him and the party set out. Lathom and his group hoped to hunt for a couple of days and then to follow that up with a day of fishing on Lower Kootenay Lake. They first made their way south to Goat Mountain. Riding along the west side of the lake, they soon crossed the narrow stretch that joined the two larger lakes. The expedition then curled around the northeastern reaches of Upper Kootenay Lake. When the mountain was in sight, they headed south. The trip was only a short 10 kilometers but distance proved to be relative. The members of the hunting party were tenderfeet, and what was for Brown a casual ride proved for them more of an adventure. As it turned out, the hunt was unsuccessful. The largest game spotted was a coyote and the only food taken was a jackrabbit, shot by Brown. The party made a night of it in the shadows of Goat Mountain, where the disappointment of the failed hunt was likely tempered with stories from Brown's great repertoire of adventures.

"Boys, that mountain over there reminds me of a sad tale," he began, pointing his finger to the east. "The highest peak in that range is called Sofa Mountain. You can't tell from this angle, but believe you me, the name aptly describes the summit. It looks like one big, old comfy chair."

He glanced at a shower of sparks from the campfire. "The Blackfoot call the region the Land of the Shining Mountains, and it can be as beautiful as the name suggests. But nature can be fearful in these parts, and when it is, that shine can mask awful terror." He gazed at his audience.

"A few years back, a Kootenay Indian was out hunting near Sofa Mountain. He had better luck than us. At least it started out that way when he found a fresh trail of a couple of mountain sheep. He followed them about halfway up the mountain before he finally brought them down. Now, it's the practice of the Indians that the men hunt and the women clean," Brown explained, "so he returned to camp, and the next day, he went back up with two women. While they were busy skinning and cutting up the kill, the Kootenay found more tracks. He left the women and continued on up the east side of the mountain. While he was gone, a freak snowstorm hit suddenly. It covered the mountain like an igloo and the temperatures fell like a stone," said Brown.

"With no warning?" asked Lathom.

"In the mountains, the weather can change faster than the time it takes to load and fire a Winchester," answered Brown. "The next day I was asked to lead a search party. I knew there was little hope, but I agreed to lead a party of six Indians up the mountain. We found the two women dead, embraced under the bloody and ragged sheepskins for warmth. We continued on and soon found the other Indian, also dead. In front of him was a pathetic collection of twigs and boughs that he had tried to use as kindling for a fire. The few matches he'd had with him were burnt out on the ground. He must have known what Mother Nature had in store for him, and it looked as if he had desperately tried to beat her to the punch by shooting himself with his rifle. A rifle's not ideally suited for that kind of work, and you could tell by looking at his body that he'd made a messy job of it. For all his effort, the cold got him, just like it did the women. We brought him back to where the women were and built a stone cairn around all three."

Brown was silent for a moment.

"Yup," he concluded, "there's great pleasure in these mountains, but there's great sorrow, too. *Ecce signum.*"

"'Look at the proof,' indeed, Brown," Lathom translated. "I, for one, will never again view these mountains in quite the same way."

A few of the men nodded in agreement, while the odd grunt of concurrence was also heard. They called it a night, and each went off to contemplate nature's unpredictable and merciless ways.

After breakfast the following morning, it was time to pack up and return to the lake. Brown watched as the greenhorn packers attempted to secure the goods for their departure. With a chuckle and a shake of his head, he moved in to take over.

"Boys," he stated, "there's a right way and a wrong way to pack a cayuse. Now, don't take offence. I've seen plenty of people do it wrong, but I've never seen it done quite as wrong as this."

The men made way for him. Brown repacked one of the bags and hoisted it up on the horse.

"The trick to doing this," Brown began, "is to make sure the pack moulds to the cayuse's body. Then you pull the cinch as tight as you can."

Brown grabbed the strap with both hands and put his whole body into tightening the strap. As he did, the strap broke and he fell to the ground, striking his head on a rock. With blood flowing, Brown embarked on a journey into the colorful world of blasphemy the likes of which these well-bred folk had likely never encountered. The words collected and formed a blue cloud above him, the hue of which made the sky pale in comparison. He finally stopped, not for lack of unused vocabulary, but to recharge his lungs. Lathom, who had been nearby, took the opportunity to come closer.

"My good man," he began, with a sparkle in his eyes. "I don't suppose you would be so kind as to again share those thoughts with us?"

The fishing proved no more successful. But despite the trip's disappointing outcome, Brown had obviously made an impression. Before departing, Brown gave Lathom an arrowhead he had collected after his experience with the Blackfoot in southern Alberta. It wasn't the last time he served as a guide for the Oxley men.

Brown also served as a guide for a future prime minister of Canada, Mackenzie Bowell, under somewhat different circumstances. At the time Minister of Customs, Bowell embarked on a tour of custom posts throughout western Canada in late 1890. By then, Brown had lived in the region for more than a decade, and it was common knowledge that there was no one better suited to guide such a tour. His services were secured in Fort Macleod and he was charged with guiding the party to Revelstoke, British Columbia, via the Crowsnest Pass.

He guided no ordinary group. Rare was it that such a powerful political figure from eastern Canada found himself in these parts. His position demanded a seven-man police escort, and in total Brown found himself guiding a party of nine with 22 animals. The trip lasted some two weeks, and Brown performed his duties in a manner that brought no complaint.

When Mackenzie Bowell embarked on his tour, Brown was still one of only a small handful of homesteaders in the lakes area. While the dramatic changes that gave new direction to the development of the prairie west were still on the horizon, the thoughtful Brown was already concerned with conservation. Even if the ranchers did not continue to expand their holdings deeper into the foothills, settlement was inevitable. Brown was well aware that Banff had recently become a national park, and it is likely that he took this opportunity to make the case for a similar future for the Kootenay Lakes. The trail from Fort Macleod took the

Sir Mackenzie Bowell (1823–1917) was born in England, his strict Protestant upbringing instilling a hatred of Liberals and Catholics in him at an early age. After immigrating to Canada in 1833, he became the owner/editor of the *Belleville Intelligencer*. Over the years he developed the reputation as a political fixer and in 1867 he was elected as a Conservative to the House of Commons, representing North Hastings. He became a senator in 1892, retiring in 1906. He held several important Cabinet portfolios, including Canadian Minister of Customs, and Trade and Commerce. After the death of Sir John Thompson in 1894, Bowell became prime minister. His term did not last long, though, as many questioned his leadership in the face of such issues as the Manitoba Schools Question. His forced resignation came on April 27, 1896. Although not politically active after his resignation, Bowell led the Opposition in the Senate from 1896 to 1906. He died from pneumonia on December 10, 1917.

party north of the region, and the majesty of the Rockies could not have failed to impress Mackenzie Bowell. Brown no doubt volunteered his opinion that the beauty of the Kootenay Lakes region made other vistas suffer in comparison. It hardly seems coincidence that when the Dominion government passed an Order in Council in 1895 creating the Kootenay Forest Reserve (a small holding that did not include the lakes themselves), Mackenzie Bowell was prime minister.

7

THE ROCKY MOUNTAIN RANGERS
1882-90

FORT MACLEOD was trying to slip the grip of winter. It was March, but the wind still had a nasty bite to it. Things warmed up pretty fast when a rider exploded into town.

"Métis attack at Duck Lake yesterday! Police killed! Louis Riel and Gabriel Dumont victorious. Rebellion! Rebellion! The Métis are up in arms. Indians likely to join forces. Rebellion!"

Crowds quickly gathered on the streets and in the bars of the Mountie town. Everyone talked of the insurrection. Ever since Métis emissaries had persuaded Louis Riel to return from exile in Montana some months earlier, the consensus had been that violence was inevitable. The Métis remembered Riel's successful leadership during the Red River Rebellion of 1869–70 in Manitoba, and they were confident that he could achieve similar results in Saskatchewan. Upon his arrival, Riel began negotiations with the Dominion government. Though there were grudging offers of land rights protection, Riel saw it as insufficient. In the face of growing numbers of English Protestant settlers, he wanted assurances that Métis cultural rights would be safeguarded. When these were not quickly forthcoming, the Métis settled on violence as the best option. They would give no quarter in their battle for a Métis homeland. The first blow was struck at Duck Lake, in the District of Saskatchewan, on March 26, 1885. Gabriel Dumont, Riel's military commander, led Métis forces in an assault on some 100 settlers, killing 12 and wounding many more.

While the settlers of southern Alberta were concerned about the Métis actions, the possibility of Native participation dominated discussion. The population of Fort Macleod was in the low hundreds, a number pretty much equal to that of the local Métis. However, the nearby Blackfoot and Blood population numbered in the thousands, not including the thousands more just south of the American border. The great fear was that the Native peoples would decide to join forces with their Métis cousins. The fear became palpable when news reached town of the Cree attack on Frog Lake, northwest of Duck Lake, on April 2. After the long winter, the poverty caused by a Dominion government policy designed to starve the Natives into submission had taken its toll. However, many of the Cree were hardly submissive; if anything, the starvation tactics had whetted their desire for self-determining action. At Frog Lake, Wandering Spirit led a small renegade band of incensed Cree warriors on the offensive. The supplies of the local Hudson's Bay Company post were pilfered and nine people were killed, including two priests. Might this be the spark that would set off a large-scale Native war?

The answer to this history-shaping question largely rested in the collective wisdom of the Native chiefs. Under the leadership of Big Bear, the Cree were hesitant. He had advised Wandering Spirit against the raid on Frog Lake but had been ignored. Government policy had at

Louis Riel gained fame as the leader of the Métis during both the Red River and North-West Rebellions. In 1869–70, he led rebels who felt their rights would not be recognized after the transfer of Hudson's Bay Company territory to Canada. Riel's provisional government successfully negotiated the Manitoba Act with the government in Ottawa, establishing the original borders of Manitoba and securing language rights for Métis in the region. Unfortunately, Riel's decision to execute English agitator Thomas Scott in 1870 forever marred his political career in Canada. While in exile in the U.S. after the Red River Rebellion, Riel was elected by his people to the House of Commons on three separate occasions but was never able to take his seat. He returned to Canada in 1884 when the Métis along the Saskatchewan requested he present their grievances to the Canadian government. Riel set up another provisional government and the North-West Rebellion began. This rebellion ended in Riel's capture. He was tried for treason in a Regina court and hanged on November 16, 1885.

least been successful in driving wedges into Native decision making. Much depended on the decision of the
Blackfoot chief, Crowfoot. His choice to participate would
bring the thousands of Blackfoot in southern Alberta into
the fray and, despite the long enmity between Blackfoot
and Cree, it was also likely to draw upon those Cree who
had decided that their future was best served with a raised
tomahawk. Crowfoot was a realist who recognized that
while the numbers of white settlers in the region were few,
their arrival in far greater numbers was inevitable.
Eventually, he decided to put his faith in the treaty that he
had helped to negotiate in 1877, and he chose the peace
pipe. The white residents of southern Alberta, however,
were not willing to sit idly by and wait for his decision.
They took matters into their own hands.

The news of the rebellion quickly reached Ottawa. As it
happened, John Stewart, a rancher from southern Alberta
who had a pocketful of military and policing credentials, was
in the Canadian capital visiting family. He quickly drew up a
defense proposal for A.P. Caron, the Minister for Militia and
Defense. Stewart suggested that a volunteer mounted unit of
150 men be raised. Caron's consent was immediate, and he
directed Stewart to establish a force based on his proposal.
Before Stewart left for Fort Macleod, he wired the town to
authorize the process of enlistment. By the time he reached
home he had been promoted to major.

Thus were the origins of the Rocky Mountain Rangers.
Eventually, three of the troops were renamed and placed
under the command of others. The fourth troop, out of the
southwestern corner of what is now Alberta, remained
known as the Number One Troop of the Rocky Mountain
Rangers and continued under Stewart's command.

The Rocky Mountain Rangers were modeled on both
the Canadian cavalry and the North-West Mounted Police.

Discipline, drill and general maintenance were governed by cavalry regulations. Because action against the Natives was fully expected, the men were also to provide their own weapons. The well-armed Ranger was expected to have a revolver, a rifle and a cartridge belt with knife attached, which reflected the Mountie's standard gear.

The dress of officers was to be that of cavalry officers, privately supplied. Troopers might be equipped with some apparel, but for the most they were to provide their own serviceable western wear. Whether potential volunteers knew that is unlikely, as suggested by the story of Rattlesnake Jack. He volunteered for duty dressed in an attractive buckskin shirt, with two commanding revolvers strapped to his chest. His appearance motivated others to join, simply because they thought his was the standard dress! Rattlesnake Jack aside, for most men customary dress consisted of a broad-brimmed felt hat, worn as the individual chose, a flannel shirt with neckerchief, and buckskin pants with Mexican-style boots. These demands did not impede enlistment in the least—the equipment and apparel mirrored the belongings of any self-respecting cowboy.

By the time of first muster, on April 15, there were some 115 volunteers. Considered by all to be a good response, especially given the short time line, the high numbers were made possible not just as a result of the desire of the locals to get involved, but because of a dramatic change in Dominion government policy regarding enlistees. Traditionally, one had to be a British citizen to serve in any Canadian militia. However, there were so many willing American cowboys in southern Alberta that this requirement had to be waived. The temporary militia unit patrolled the area bounded by High River in the north, Medicine Hat in the east, and the international boundary in the south. The absence of a western patrol indicated that there was little fear of any attack through the

In response to the North-West Rebellion of 1885, Ottawa authorized the formation of a volunteer mounted unit of 150 men to protect southern Alberta from the potential fallout of Louis Riel's and Gabriel Dumont's uprising. The Rocky Mountain Rangers were modeled on both the Canadian cavalry and the North-West Mounted Police. The pay for officers was equal to that of a Canadian cavalry officer, ranging from 90¢ to $1.50 a day. Troopers received the equivalent pay of a North-West Mounted Police constable, about 75¢ a day. All men received allowances for food and for the use of a horse, which enlistees were required to provide. A Mexican saddle, bridle and lariat were also standard issue. Men were expected to provide their own weapons, with the well-armed Ranger having a revolver, a rifle and a cartridge belt with a knife. Customary dress included a broad-brimmed felt hat, worn as the individual chose, a flannel shirt with neckerchief and buckskin pants with Mexican-style boots.

Rocky Mountains. The "Tough Men," as the locals fondly called the Rangers, were responsible for maintaining telegraph wires and Canadian Pacific Railway track, protecting cattle herds from those men low enough to take advantage of the crisis and, most importantly, ensuring that Natives from below the 49th parallel did not journey north to join in arms. On April 29, the Rangers began their patrol, riding east from Fort Macleod. They were to become a chapter of the storied tradition of law and order on the Canadian prairies.

෨෬

Deep in the mountains, Brown was unaware of unfolding events. It was always his practice to hunt in the spring of the year, but 1885 saw him leave home early, while heavy snow still bent the boughs of the firs. Brown had his own problems and they were serious enough to demand the strongest of remedies, which for him meant the solitude provided by the open air and mountains. Olivia, his beloved wife, had recently died and he had given up his children to be raised by others. At age 46, Brown had sustained many injuries over the years. He could count among them broken bones and arrow-pierced flesh. But he came to discover that there was no pain to compare with the suffering of loss, especially when he held himself responsible. The booze did not help this time, though he had given it a good try over the winter. The cabin held too many memories. Alone, in nature…that was the only way to ease his guilt.

Olivia had not been a physically strong woman, and she had found the pioneering life along the shores of the Kootenay Lakes demanding. The birth of their third child and only son, Leo, in 1882, was difficult and left her weak. She never fully recovered from the debilitating labor. Brown, however, also saw the slow spiritual decline that had left Olivia sapped and susceptible. As a Métis, Olivia had been raised in an environment where family and community were the foundations of life. Brown took her from that, and they had withdrawn deep into an isolated world where visitors were few. Her people were hundreds of kilometers away on the plains. Brown's work as a guide, trader and trapper often took him away for extended periods. She had never complained, but Brown saw the toll taken by the loneliness. Brown himself had felt paralyzed. He found meaning in nature, a meaning he could best experience alone. Unfortunately, his need for solitude must have been a contributing factor in Olivia's decline.

The immediate circumstances of Olivia's death were harrowing, and they sunk Brown into the deepest of depressions. He had ridden off, saying he was going to drop in on one of the local Mountie detachments. There was no reason for the visit; there never was. Brown just liked to loaf around. He had been gone a few days when Olivia died. Luckily for the children, Brown had a hired man to do the work around the cabin. The following days saw that poor man busy trying to keep the children away from their mother's lifeless body. Terror reigned as the children begged to know why their pleas to their mother to wake up went unanswered. The hired man prayed for Brown's return. When several more days passed, he realized it was necessary to do something about the decomposing body. He collected some wood from around the place and fashioned a coffin amidst the screams of the perplexed children.

"Leave mama alone!" they cried.

He obeyed their wishes only after he had buried Olivia.

Brown finally returned. He was confused when the children ran to him and shouted that their mother was gone. All was clear after he met with the hired hand.

"I kept her as long as I could, Mr. Brown. She's gone now. There's nothing I could do. Her last words were for you to be kind to the children and to make sure they get an education." With that, the man burst into tears and ran off. "I never again want to see such sorrow!" he cried.

With Olivia gone, Brown saw the raising of his three children as an undesirable task. While the oldest girl, who was entering her teenage years, was old enough to be responsible for the domestic duties of the household, the boy was still a toddler and Brown probably rationalized that one so small was ill-suited for a life in the woods. More to the point, the children would shackle his preferred lifestyle. Soon after Olivia died, he headed into Fort Macleod, where he sought out the prominent Catholic missionary Father Lacombe for advice. Because Brown was an Anglican by birth, his choice of advisors might seem a bit odd. However, by this time in his life, Brown had all but rejected formal religion and was well on his way to adopting Theosophy, an orientation that fit better with his views on individuality, materialism and nature. Besides, Father Lacombe was a respected friend, and Olivia herself had been raised as a Catholic. The priest recommended that the boy be sent to the church's convent school outside St. Albert, near Edmonton. When he grew older, Leo moved to Athabasca Landing, Alberta, where he remained in contact with his father. Lacombe's advice as to the girls has not been recorded, though Brown also gave them up at about this time. By early April 1885 Brown was back at his cabin, alone, the pain of his choices dulled but still present.

It was about this time that Jack Street, a long-time hunting partner and friend, made his way out to the Brown homestead for an unexpected visit. Street was a member of the North-West Mounted Police who was stationed nearby; he had come to be a welcome caller as he went on his rounds. When Brown was hired by the Mounties to break horses, he and Street met often. The two had hit it off from the start and spent many a day hunting and prospecting through the mountains, or just enjoying the scenery. As he approached the cabin, Street heard Brown long before he saw him. Brown was deep into one of his rants, using language strong enough to peel the bark from a tree. As a Mountie, Street had encountered the lowest of the low, so foul language was hardly unfamiliar to him. But Brown's skill was that of an artist—when he really got going, even Street felt like blushing. The Mountie reached the edge of the clearing, where he saw Brown taking a stick to a black bear. Not as big as its grizzly relative, the black bear was nonetheless one of nature's more imposing forces. Brown placed every bit of strength from his wiry body into the whupping, pausing only to catch his breath.

"A good workout, eh, Kootenai?" Street called.

Brown's head popped up as if it was pulled by a string.

"Damn bear," he said. "I was low on firewood and wanted to haul some up here from down by lake's end. That bear's been gone for days, and I had to do it myself."

Street realized that this bear was the one that Brown had raised from a cub and trained as a pack animal. Brown threw the stick down at the feet of the cowering animal and walked to the cabin. Street led his horse over to the hitching post and tied it up. As he left it, the horse became skittish, snorting loudly and repeatedly. Street looked around to determine the problem. There, at the opposite edge of the clearing, was another bear.

"Looks like we got some more company, Kootenai," said Street, as he pulled his rifle from the sheath attached to his saddle and indicated the bear with a tilt of his head.

Brown looked over to where his friend had signaled. He motioned to Street to lower the rifle. Brown cocked his head to the right, an action repeated by the bear. He then squinted one eye and raised the brow of the other. Street watched the bear. If he had had to testify in court, he would have sworn the animal did the same thing, except it didn't have eyebrows.

After a moment's silence and consideration, Brown called out the name of his pet bear. "Healy?"

Slowly and submissively, the bear trotted over. Both men looked over to the discarded stick and saw the wild bear scampering off into the woods. Brown simply shook his head, while Street had a good laugh.

"I'll put the kettle on," Brown said finally. "What's the news from town?"

"It hardly beats the story I'll be able tell to folks now," chuckled Street. "Kootenai Brown, fearless mountain man, taking on wild bears with nothing more than a strong piece of willow!"

Brown scowled. They made their way into the cabin, and as they sat at a roughly hewn homemade table, Street related the news of the rebellion and the Rocky Mountain Rangers. Before they finished their coffee, Brown had decided to offer his services. He was not much on being ordered around anymore, but joining the troop would give him something to focus on and thereby help him to forget the recent painful events. Brown might also have felt the tug of the memories of his days with the British Army and thought that serving with the Rangers could be a way to relive old times. By evening, he and Street were riding back to town together.

ॐ

Upon arriving in Fort Macleod, Brown made inquiries into the Rangers. Because he knew most of the ranchers in the region, it is likely he made his way to Major John Stewart, who had himself just arrived back in town. Brown offered his services and left it to the commanding officer to determine how his skills might best be put to use. By the time their meeting ended, Brown had been signed up as chief scout, at a trooper's salary. Brown's enlistment was something of a coup. He had lived in the region for so long that he qualified as an old-timer. His knowledge of the land was unsurpassed, and his experiences certainly qualified him for his new duties. The local news heralded Brown's addition to the troop as a valuable one. His presence in the Rocky Mountain Rangers must have brought confidence to the men, many of whom were green to military work. His campfire stories of his past exploits would prove to be a great source of entertainment, introducing some spice to what was, for the most part, an uneventful tour of duty.

Having served in the British military, which prided itself on order and subordination, Brown must have enjoyed quite a few chuckles while watching the men drill. As cowboys, the Rangers were an independent lot, used to following their own lead. That they had trouble falling into line when directed was not a mark of disrespect to the officers, but only suggestive of their own easygoing ways. Unusual indeed was the exercise that was not interrupted by the cowboys' free-spirited hijinks. On one occasion, as the men were being paraded through town, a trooper peeled off in the general direction of a local watering hole. When an officer commanded him to stop and state his intent, the man looked back over his shoulder and casually replied, "Not t' worry, sir. I'll catch up with you fellers a'fore long."

The Rocky Mountain Rangers are shown here in formation with Kootenai Brown in the lead. They patrolled the region from High River in the north to Medicine Hat in the east and the U.S. border to the south. They did not patrol the western reaches of the region close to the Rockies since an attack was unlikely from that quarter.

Training for the rangers was minimal. It was understood that frontier defense required a certain independent approach to be effective. These were men used to the inconveniences of frontier work, men who would drink out of their hats if there was no cup and who would feel comfortable using the shelter of a saddle on a rough night. Furthermore, the officers knew that they were not going to be able to turn sow's ears into silk purses, no matter how much they drilled.

By the end of April, training was complete and the Rangers began to make their way east. Over the next week, they passed through Lethbridge, where some of the men remained, and then Medicine Hat. Another part of the troop continued on to the Cypress Hills, near the District of Saskatchewan, while the rest began their border patrol. It was the start of a relatively unexciting three months when the daily routine was to march along the invisible line separating Canada and the U.S. As it turned out, the border wasn't the only thing invisible. There was little evidence of Natives, a source of much discontent to many of the men who had signed on fully expecting—and even *wanting*—to fight. There was a report of a Native attack on a lone cattleman in the Medicine Hat area, but by the time the Rangers arrived, any Natives had long since vamoosed. So rare was any encounter that when one of the troopers finally did see a Native, not one among the Rangers believed his story. His reputation under attack, this man—a scout under Brown—set out to prove his case by gathering some brush and sending up smoke signals. As the smoke drifted up against the clear blue sky, an answer in like form was promptly received from a group several kilometers away. The Rangers took off in quick pursuit, but upon arrival they found the site abandoned. The departed Natives were untraceable. At a later date, Stewart reported to a local newspaper that shots had been exchanged with a group of 30 to 40 Natives, but the gunplay proved uneventful.

The monotony of patrolling was punctuated by the evening gathering around the campfire, about the only source of entertainment the men had during their duty. If the troopers could not actually experience action, they could live it vicariously through the stories of seasoned veterans like Brown, who was constantly urged to share his experiences of days gone by. Seated around a popping fire that sent sparks into the dusky night, smoking pipes and rolled cigarettes, or simply chewing tobacco, and warmed by grainy cups from a bottomless pot of coffee, the men would quietly sit, enraptured.

"In the spring of '65, me and my pals gave up our gold-mining claims along the Wild Horse Creek in the Cariboo and set out for Fort Edmonton," Brown began one story. "It was at that time that I first saw Kootenay Lakes. As we emerged from the foothills onto the plains, we all knew we were entering into Blackfoot country. We didn't know what to expect. Remember, back in those days there were just a few white men—missionaries like Father Lacombe—until you reached Edmonton. The towns we see now on the prairies weren't even dreams then! It's not like the Blackfoot knew much about our kind, and we knew even less about them, save for their war-like ways." He took a swig of coffee.

"We stopped near Seven Persons' Creek and bedded down for the night in the shelter of a clump of cotton-woods. Our bedrolls weren't even warm before a shower of arrows rained down upon us. We had met our first Blackfoot war party. The five of us went diving for cover among the trees and, brother, let me tell you that every last one of us thought we had reached the end." Brown shuddered at the memory.

"There were some 30 young bucks in all, and they were out for bear. The Blackfoot rode bareback and used a rawhide halter that went through the horse's mouth. They didn't have any guns, but I can assure you they made the most of those arrows. They soon flushed us out of the trees and we made for the ridge of a coulee, where there was some low-lying brush. As we ran, we fired our rifles wildly at anything that moved. It was slow going, though, because we were using old muzzle-loaders with balls and caps. Our pockets and mouths were full of spare bullets. It was more luck than skill that brought down two of their party," Brown admitted.

"Soon they tired of the game and moved on, stripping buck naked and swimming across the Saskatchewan, but not before one of their arrows found its mark in my side, just above my kidney. I feared that was it for me. I'm not much on God, but I prayed for His forgiveness as I clutched the arrow's shaft with two hands and gave it a sharp tug. My flesh burned as the obsidian point ripped out through the small hole. It was over two inches long, it turned out—I still have it. It might as well have been two feet long. In those days we had no medicine, so we had to use our imagination when dealing with injury. I brought out a bottle of turpentine and got one of my pals to do the doctoring. I bent over while he popped the cork and put the neck of the bottle into the opening left by the arrowhead. I think he poured about half a pint of the vile stuff into the wound, and I don't know that the pain caused by that wasn't worse than the arrow itself," Brown winced. "It must have been good medicine, though, because within a few days, the pain had gone, the wound had healed up and the injury never again bothered me."

The next day Brown took some of the men down near the river where they had camped. They found two Native skulls and dug five balls from the towering cottonwoods. Brown hadn't told his companions the night before, but they were camped at the very spot where his adventure had unfolded.

Apparently the only real action Brown saw during his tour with the Rangers involved a pair of horse rustlers. The troop received word that two men were on their way up from Montana with a band of 16 horses. Suspicions were raised because the men were avoiding the regular trails.

Reports indicated that the men were traveling east of Fort Macleod, but moving in a westerly direction toward the foothills of the Rockies. Given his extensive knowledge of the mountains, Brown was the logical choice to accompany two Mounties who had been assigned the job of bringing the men in. The trio tracked the suspected rustlers up as far as the community of High River, finally intercepting them along the banks of the Highwood River. After some searching downstream, the rustlers' cache of horses was discovered. The men were arrested for smuggling stolen horses into Canada and were brought to justice in Fort Macleod. Although the event had nothing to do with the rebellion, it reflected the Rangers' mandate to generally maintain law and order in the region.

෴

The Rocky Mountain Rangers were recalled to Fort Macleod in early July 1885 after the rebellion petered out. Having signed on to fight the Natives and eagerly anticipating numerous bloody encounters, the men were disappointed. Local residents, however, valued the Rangers' contributions for what they were. The troop had protected the cattle country and their patrols had ensured that the violence didn't have a chance to spread farther west. The townspeople recognized the troop with a parade and a formal ball. At the front of the troop, riding abreast of Major Stewart, Kootenai Brown basked in the town's gratitude. He was no longer much on formal affairs, though, and he chose to visit friends rather than participate in the ball.

Although Stewart exerted efforts to have the Rangers made into a permanent militia troop, the Dominion government was uninterested. So, with the praise and thanks of numerous town dignitaries, the Rangers disbanded and the men resumed their pre-rebellion activities. Life returned to normal. For their efforts, the men were given the Riel (or North-West) Rebellion medal. Brown's was inscribed "J.G. Brown, Chief Scout, Rocky Mountain Rangers." The men also received rebellion scrip, which amounted to either $80 or 320 acres of land. Brown applied for the latter and came to own a second homestead in the Kootenay region. For his 77 days of work, Brown pocketed just under $120. But his main motivation was not financial. As he later told a friend, he was more interested in drinking Jamaica Ginger and having a good time!

Brown returned to his original homestead and slipped back into a comfortable life that followed the familiar rhythms of nature. He made no effort to develop his second homestead, preferring to use it for grazing cattle and horses. Over the winter, he frequently visited nearby residents. Popular destinations included the local North-West Mounted Police detachments and the nearby Cochrane Ranch. Brown occasionally journeyed into town. Upon such visits, a local reporter regularly sought Brown out and duly recorded for the newspaper Brown's views on fishing and hunting. Brown's home was also open to any of the travelers who might journey by—the door was swung wide and the pot put on the stove. More often than not, however, the long winter nights found Brown engrossed in one of the many classical books that filled his home library. A typical night might find him reading Tennyson, Shakespeare or one of the ancient Greek or Latin authors. Some folks referred to Brown as a mountain man, but the label hardly did him justice—it gave no indication of his lifelong love for learning and his penchant for deep and considered reflection on intellectual matters.

This medal was awarded to soldiers taking part in the suppression of the North-West Rebellion of 1885, but was given only to those who had served west of Port Arthur. North-West Mounted Police were excluded from receiving the medal until 1900, when those members who had served in the campaign were given the medalion. The circular silver medal was 1.41 inches in diameter. Its plain straight suspender is attached with a double-toe claw and is a gray ribbon with crimson stripes. The medal was authorized on July 24, 1885 and issued on September 18, 1885. In total, 5650 medals were issued.

All was not rosy during this period of Brown's life. The wound caused by the loss of his family still festered, and it took a physical toll. In the spring of 1886, Brown fell gravely ill. For a homesteader, especially a single one isolated from settlement, sickness was a serious matter. Brown was confined to bed, mostly lost in the delirious netherworld between dreams and reality. If it had not been for the timely appearance of Willie Cochrane, proprietor of the nearby ranch, who decided to drop in on his friend while in search of some lost cattle, the story of Kootenai Brown would be much shorter. In true pioneer spirit, Cochrane abandoned his search for the lost animals and quickly made his way to Fort Macleod. Once there, he successfully impressed the seriousness of the situation on George Kennedy local doctor and assistant surgeon for the police detachment. They returned to Brown's cabin together. Kennedy, a good friend of Brown's, determined that there was little to be done for the sick man without a proper medical environment. Together the men transported Brown back to town. Each of these journeys was nearly 100 kilometers, traveled on horseback over often difficult terrain. Their efforts demonstrated the depth of frontier friendship. As a result of his service with the Rocky Mountain Rangers, and his relationships with Cochrane and Kennedy, Brown was brought to the local North-West Mounted Police hospital, where he was treated.

After being slowly nursed back to health, Brown spent the following weeks recuperating at his cabin. The illness had been a sobering affair and undoubtedly gave him cause for reflection. He enjoyed his journeys into the mountains, where he could reflect on matters of deep spiritual interest, and he had little difficulty feeding his considerable physical appetites when in town. But experience had taught him of the risks of a solitary life. At best, they were unnecessary— at worst, dangerous.

Here is Brown seated in the right foreground in front of his cabin on Lower Kootenay Lake in October 1883. The picture was taken for a book entitled *From Home to Home* by A. Stavely Hill (seated at left). The other man in the picture is not identified, but having so many visitors at a time was rare in the early days of homesteading in the West. There were likely three visitors, including the photographer.

Brown greatly admired the way the Métis constructed both their camps and their homes. Brown modeled his Kootenay home on Métis cabin design, but it is clear he made some modifications to the design to suit himself. Most Métis cabins relied on their huge fireplaces for their source of illumination. For this cabin, however, Brown obviously went to the great trouble and expense of having glass windows freighted in and installed.

It was at about this time that a party of Cree from Saskatchewan happened by Brown's cabin. Trading provided an important part of Brown's livelihood, and Natives from near and far came to do business with him. The group rode into his clearing, in search of Inuspi, Brown's Native name, which translated as "Long Hair." As Brown strode out of his cabin with hair flowing over his shoulders, the Cree knew they had found the man for whom they searched.

"Inuspi, we have come to trade," said the leader of the party. "We have many hides."

Brown sized up the party. They numbered about a dozen. One in particular, a young and shy woman, immediately struck Brown's fancy. When his mind was set, Brown was not a man to mince words.

"Sure," Brown replied to them in Cree. "We can do some trading. Let's start with my offer. I'll give you five cayuses for the squaw," he offered, pointing to his chosen one. Part of Brown's income came from breaking wild horses and then selling them. They were a valuable currency.

"Ungh," the Cree leader grunted. "You mean Chee-pay-tha-qua-ka-soon?" This was the Cree word for "Blue Flash of Lightning." The girl bowed her head.

"Yup," Brown responded.

The Cree men huddled together and agreed the payment was fair. Before long, Brown had his second wife.

The trading continued on through the afternoon. As was often the case, the goods exchanged included some firewater, though not too much—the last thing Brown wanted to see was an armed Native devoid of self-control. Brown's firewater was no doubt the standard mixture of tobacco, copper sulfate and red ink with a dash of Tabasco. The ink left the telltale red moustache, and there was always just enough booze to pass the fire test. When a few drops were poured on a fire, they went up in a burst of flame. All in all, it was potent stuff. When the dealing was done, the Cree broke open the liquid, as was their practice. On this occasion, as the Cree became tipsy, an idea came to Brown. He was fond of gambling, and he shrewdly saw that a possibility for a tidy profit had emerged.

"I've got a proposition," he said to the Cree leader. "How about we have a pony race?"

It was not the first time Brown had offered such a suggestion, since he enjoyed these competitions so much.

Competitions of skill were also a magnet to the Natives. They loved to compare their abilities with those of others. As they looked at this wild-haired man, they must have thought that the pickings would be easy. They readily agreed to the contest, unaware that Brown's somewhat comical looks concealed his excellent frontier skills. He would have stood a good chance of winning even if the Cree hadn't been drinking.

"Now boys," Brown continued, "a race isn't exciting without a prize. How about five cayuses to the winner?"

The Cree accepted the terms and selected their contestant. Unsteadily, the man mounted his horse. Together, he and Brown marked out the trail to be followed. Finally they sat abreast—Brown on his chestnut horse, the Cree on his smaller pinto—and waited for Chee-pay-tha-qua-ka-soon to give the cue to start. At her signal, they were off into the woods. Some minutes later, Brown reemerged, barreling past the finish line. Only later did the Cree, who had apparently fallen off his horse, follow.

As the cayuses were exchanged, the Cree began to grumble, and Brown slowly placed his right hand on the butt of the Colt .45 that rarely left his side. He slipped it out of the holster and pointed it in the direction of the group of Cree. At this point, Brown was not sure whether the Cree would be more of a threat drunk or sober, but he

Like many men in the days of the early West, Brown took a Native wife.
Chee-pay-tha-qua-ka-soon, shown here, adopted the English name of
Isabella, though Brown took to calling her *Nichemoos*, the Cree word for
"dear." Father Lacombe later solemnized their marriage. Although they
endured some difficult times. Brown and Isabella eventually became
great partners. She was comfortable with Brown's absences, which
proved to be fewer for her than they had been for Olivia. Though she
was a small woman, barely reaching the shoulders of Brown's 5'8"
frame, Nichemoos was strong and her skills around the campfire made
her an invaluable companion on his hunting trips.

was sure that he would be better off seeing the rumps of their horses disappearing into the woods. The Cree got the message, and, in the face of Brown's cool demeanor and apparent willingness to move beyond words, packed up and left. The last they saw of Chee-pay-tha-qua-ka-soon was a quick glimpse back at her standing dutifully behind Brown.

THE LEGEND GROWS
THE 1890S

HIS TOUR OF DUTY with the Rocky Mountain Rangers completed, the newly married Brown settled into a routine very much like his pre-rebellion days. As a frontiersman, Brown's income derived from a variety of sources. He guided, trapped, fished and offered his services on a contract basis. It was a lifestyle that saw him involved in virtually all the events that were associated with the development of the West. He worked for the North-West Mounted Police, participated in early mineral exploration, and contracted his services to the Canadian Pacific Railway. By the 1890s, he was actively advocating the preservation of the Kootenay region as a reserve and, once successful, for its expansion. But Brown wasn't shackled to frontier life. Town, especially Fort Macleod, served as a useful distraction to the demands of homesteading. And perhaps it is misleading to suggest that Brown's urban pursuits were mere distractions; he regularly found necessary stimulation and great pleasure in the amenities Fort Macleod offered. But town wasn't the only place where the pulse could be quickened.

When there was money to be made, and authorities to be duped, he was not shy about breaking the law. In fact, it was during this period that Brown was one of the many whisky smugglers who illegally imported booze from the United States.

Given the manner by which Brown occasionally made a living, it is indeed ironic that he also found employment with the North-West Mounted Police. Whether whisky smuggling or bartering firewater a little too freely with Natives, Brown was more often on the run *from* the men in scarlet than he was running *with* them. As it turns out, Brown never worked as a policeman in the force. Instead, he opened packing routes for the Mounties. On one occasion, this duty brought him into contact with the unbending Superintendent Sam Steele. Following the North-West Rebellion, Steele was directed to Wild Horse Creek to assist in pacifying the resident Kootenay Natives. Brown was called out to his old stomping grounds to cache provisions along the trail for the traveling men. Another of Brown's duties was to handle the force's horses, and he broke and pastured them on his second homestead. Brown enjoyed an ongoing love affair with horses and he was good at working them. But no man is perfect, and Brown suffered a broken leg after being thrown by one of the animals. While his leg healed, the Mounties unceremoniously dropped him from the payroll. A more long-term effect of the injury was that the broken leg, one of many such accidents, gave Brown a bowlegged appearance in later life and made him seem much shorter than his 5'8" height. Brown also provided warehousing services to the Mounties; his cabin was ideally situated as a location to store goods. Perhaps his most important function, however, was as a source of information on area terrain and routes. Brown's singular knowledge of the region ensured he was invaluable.

The North-West Mounted Police's beginnings can be found primarily in the Red River Rebellion. When Louis Riel and the Métis took action in 1869, Prime Minister John A. Macdonald found himself at a distinct disadvantage. He had no effective military presence to send to Manitoba in response. Macdonald didn't want to be caught handicapped again, so he organized the North-West Mounted Police. Initially he envisioned them as a military organization, the Mounted Riflemen, but when the United States government voiced concern about an armed force on its northern border, Macdonald relented. He craftily massaged the organization so that it appeared to be more a civilian and administrative body.

By 1874 the Mounties had successfully, and miraculously, completed their long march west. Facing physical deprivation, and often lost on the great barren prairie, they had somehow persevered. Their inauspicious beginnings did not foreshadow the impact the organization would have on the West. But with them, British justice had arrived.

The objective of the Mounties was to impose peace and order on the vast western plains. It is a tribute to the dedication and fortitude of the first Mounties that they were able to achieve that goal with fewer than 300 men. They ended the threats of the Irish nationalist Fenian raiders and effectively halted the activities of American whisky traders and wolfers. They developed good relations with the Native people, and the trust they inspired quelled many of the concerns of the indigenous population. They did their jobs so effectively that bloodshed was rare.

Brown himself worked for the Mounties for other reasons than just money. The force was the anchor that stabilized the West. While Brown was no stickler on law and order, he was sensitive about rapid and destructive change to the Kootenay Lakes region, and he likely saw the Mounties as the best hope of providing a barrier against any such an onslaught.

Brown's experiences with minerals in the region also serve to illustrate his conservationist attitude. Alberta's greatest source of financial reward has been oil. Discoveries and exploitation over the 20th century, from Turner Valley to Leduc to Fort McMurray, have filled government treasuries with funds from the sale of the black gold. Brown had his hands dirty in oil long before it became a coveted resource. In fact, a good case can be made for the claim that he was the first white man in Alberta to use it. However, Brown didn't see oil simply as a way to make a profit. Rather, he integrated it into his everyday activities.

The Kootenay Natives had long been aware of the thick black liquid that seeped from the ground in the Kootenay region. They used it primarily as a paste to treat wounds. The Natives shared their knowledge with Brown at some point in the early 1880s. The oil proved to be a valuable resource; Brown used it to grease the wheels of his wagons and as an ointment to smear on flanks of horses to prevent the merciless assault of blackflies. To a lesser degree, he also used it as a fuel. He held his information close to the vest because he was aware of the intrusions and speedy change that widespread knowledge of the resource would bring. Only when some local Native guides led curious parties to the seepage sites in the 1890s did oil interests finally began to exploit the findings.

Once Brown realized that the exploitation of oil would be inevitable, he too became a participant, though hardly in a large-scale or disruptive way. Teaming with William Aldridge, whom Brown had hired as a manual laborer, he began to collect and sell the oil, primarily for use with horses. The men used blankets to soak up the oil and then squeezed the sopping blankets dry over barrels. Given the great number of ranches in the region, the fly repellant was a product in considerable demand and it resulted in a nice income for Brown. Others, however, were not content with an operation so tiny and Luddite and wanted to introduce more modern technology. They brought in rigs, often imported from down east. The first wells were drilled in 1891. Oil was not struck until a decade later, in what was then almost literally a hole in the ground known hopefully as Oil City. The success set off a minor boom characterized by a gaggle of rough oil workers and competing interests, all of whom were often violent in their efforts to control the resource.

The organized oil exploitation was a real concern for Brown because it threatened the environment he had chosen to call home. Some might say that Brown made his own bed and that subsequent developments only forced him to sleep in it. His selling barrels of oil certainly publicized the resource's availability, and, as such, he bore some responsibility for the presence of the oil interests. But Brown's practices were not intrusive and they posed little or no threat to the region's untouched majesty. His reluctance to exploit the resource on a grander scale was in large part born of his desire to keep the area pristine. Brown was savvy enough to know the way of miners and mining companies, and he didn't want any part of them. In fact, Brown had even kept quiet his discovery of gold in the Kootenay Lakes region in the early 1890s. He brought an ore sample into the assay office at Fort Macleod, and after discovering that the sample had a large quantity of gold in it, he simply left the office and kept the location a secret. There are no records of Brown selling gold thereafter. He clearly didn't want a gold rush because a boom would inevitably mean the destruction of all he held dear. Similarly, although he could have easily staked a claim and controlled the oil deposits, he chose not to. Instead, the presence of the oil interests simply toughened Brown's determination to have the region protected as a national park. When the Kootenay district was at issue, Brown regularly opted for the stability that ensured its protection.

∽

If the North-West Mounted Police established the context for change, iron and steam made it possible. The 20th century arrived in western Canada riding an iron horse. The Canadian Pacific Railway, the fruition of Macdonald's dream of linking Canada's Atlantic and Pacific coasts, was completed in 1885. Few guessed that it would be more than a decade before the railway demonstrated its greatest value. Through the vigorous efforts of Prime Minister Wilfrid Laurier and his tireless Minister of the Interior, Clifford Sifton, the railway became a mechanism for funneling European immigrants into "the last best west" after 1896. Such was the face of progress, and it drew differing reactions from western old-timers. There were few who argued against the economic benefits that came with increasing numbers of immigrants. Settlers broke the land, turning the soil into ready cash that sustained and bolstered growth. Others, however, were uncomfortable with the rapidity of change, and they fretted over both imagined and real lawlessness and disorder.

Brown counted himself among those who lamented the effects of change. He was not a man opposed to progress. In later years, particularly, he was an advocate of development and often shared with friends his pleasure when a local business undertaking, be it logging or lake transportation, was successful. He also wanted the region to be accessible to those who shared his love of nature. However, Brown always preferred development to be orderly and he was far from convinced that it was desirable at any cost.

As someone who had witnessed dramatic change in other parts of the West, Brown knew that the construction of the Canadian Pacific Railway to the north of the Kootenay Lakes foreshadowed the changes that were to reach into his world. By the late 1890s, the reach became reality. First, a spur line extending west of Fort Macleod was built. More significant was the subsequent construction of the Crowsnest Pass Railway, a line projected to extend from Lethbridge to the Kootenays in the interior of British Columbia.

Since the gold rush days of the 1860s, Brown's old haunt around the Wild Horse Creek was the commercial hinterland of interests located in nearby Washington state. When the gold rush played out, the same companies moved into the coal business. They employed miners who extracted coal for local smelters, and then they shipped out the refined product on a local railway line that they had constructed. The industry proved profitable, but just barely. Once news of the Klondike gold discovery in northern Canada broke in 1897, the coal-mining interests sought to unburden themselves of their Kootenay millstone so that they could try for higher profits by exploiting the untold gold deposits. Their desire to exit coincided nicely with the emerging vision of Canadian Pacific Railway executives, who hoped to more fully integrate the Kootenay coal field with the larger Canadian economy. In 1898, a deal was struck whereby the Canadian Pacific Railway bought out American interests in the region.

The greatest challenge to integration was the massive cost involved in building a railway through the Rocky Mountains. The most suitable route was via the Crowsnest

Pass, but "suitable" was a relative term; the entire southern portion of the Canadian Rockies was an engineer's nightmare. The plan of the Canadian Pacific Railway, however, was characterized by foresight as much as by anticipation of profits; they had laid the groundwork for their future efforts in 1897, when they signed the Crowsnest Pass Agreement with the Dominion government. In return for massive government subsidies to aid costly construction, the company agreed to lower its freight rates on settlers' goods coming into the West and farmers' grain transported east. These were significant concessions for the government, agreed to primarily because they made immigration more attractive. In addition, the plan directed the needed coal to settlers and industries east of the Rockies.

In mid-July 1897, the first sod of the Crowsnest Pass Railway was turned in Lethbridge. One sniff of the development was enough to cause Kootenai Brown to toss his nose in the air at this initial wave of assaulting change. Construction brought strangers, and there were some rough, tough customers in the group. The laying of track required construction gangs: physical laborers who were, for the most part, recent immigrants accustomed to a hardscrabble existence. A second group of laborers soon arrived in numbers previously unseen in Fort Macleod. Miners, sensing opportunity in the Rockies, flowed into the region. They were men with purely pecuniary interests, often given to violence. Brown had endured his fill of such men during his days in the Cariboo, feeling that this immigrant vanguard was a poor foundation on which to build a community. Furthermore, the immigrants' activities disrupted the local game populations and Brown could only sadly report to the local newspapers that scarcity was increasingly commonplace. Brown felt that an open-armed reception for these folks was hardly appropriate.

Brown was nothing if not pragmatic, however, and faced
with the inevitability of the development, he figured that
he might as well take the opportunity to supplement his
income. He signed on with one of the supply contractors
engaged on the British Columbia side of the Rockies.
Brown's knowledge of the region, combined with his packing skills, made the contractor's decision to hire him an easy
one. In September 1897, Brown found himself in charge of
a pack train near Wardner. The suppliers had the weighty
responsibility of ensuring that all necessary goods were
freighted before the spring thaw, because once the break-up
occurred it was impossible to ship goods. As the leader of a
pack train, Brown's duties were relatively simple. He was
required to properly secure supplies on the pack animals
and transport them to predetermined camps, where they
would be used by the construction gangs in subsequent
months. Still, it was challenging work, and negotiating narrow and difficult trails, often little more than scratches in
mountainous terrain, was not without problems. Skittish
horses were none too pleased to be following a path that
would have tested the skills of a mountain goat. Thick
brush often made the going slow and tiring. Nonetheless,
the work was to Brown's liking. For the most part, he was
alone in nature and able to enjoy his regular pastime of
reflecting upon weighty philosophical issues. Sooner or
later, however, a pack train had to reach its destination. On
one such occasion, Brown discovered that the full load he
had packed had failed to arrive with him. A sack of beans
was empty. The camp cook was not at all pleased with the
shortfall, and a confrontation ensued.

"You're telling me, Brown, that this sack was full of
beans when you left?" asked the cook, a nasty tone of insin-
uation in his voice.

"A fully packed sack," Brown replied matter-of-factly.

"And here you are with an empty sack. How do you explain that?" demanded the cook.

Brown put one hand in the sack and poked three fingers through a hole just above the bottom seam. "Seems to me that it must've ripped somewhere along the trail," he answered. "I guess the beans spilled out."

"Do you take me for a fool, Brown? You think I'm going to believe a cockamamie story like that? Sack magically rips and spills the beans—next you'll be spouting off 'bout some giant beanstalks. You know damn well that those beans are hidden in a nice dry place somewhere along the trail," the cook stated flatly. "They're just waiting for you to pick 'em up on the way back."

"I don't like what I'm hearing," Brown replied. He did not take kindly to slurs on his honor. Nothing was more likely to kindle the short fuse of his temper than an accusation, especially if it was unwarranted. "Are you calling me a thief?"

"Damn right," snapped the cook. "If the hat fits, wear it."

"You sure as hell don't know me well enough to know my hat size, mister, and I'll be damned if I'm going to stand here and let the likes of you call me a thief," said Brown, whose hand had pushed back his jacket to give ready access to the Colt .45 revolver strapped to his side. Jaw clenched and eyes narrowed, he asked, "Would you mind repeating your thoughts on the matter?"

The unarmed cook hesitated. He was considering the consequences of rash action, when a Mr. Harvey, one of the engineers at the construction site, arrived.

"Brown, you worried that you might not be able to find your way back to town?" Harvey asked.

"What's that, Harvey?" Brown replied. The cook used the interruption as an opportunity to scurry behind the engineer.

"Well, I just rode into camp and all along the trail was the damnedest site," Harvey explained. "A trail of beans stretched along for more than a couple of miles. I heard that you were the latest packer to arrive in camp, so I figured you must have left them behind."

Brown lifted the sack that he still held in one hand and showed Harvey the hole.

"Yeah, that explains it," said Harvey. "Must've been ripped open by a tree."

"I'd say that's the only explanation," said Brown, staring at the cook.

"I agree," the cook eagerly replied. "Anybody who'd suggest otherwise is a blamed fool!"

By this time, Harvey had noticed that Brown's jacket was thrown open and tucked back behind his revolver. He placed his hand on Brown's shoulder.

"Brown, you want to take a stroll with me?" Harvey asked. "There's something I'd like to discuss."

"I think that's a good idea," replied Brown, straightening his jacket. "The cook here is going fix me some grub, but I imagine it'll take a spell."

"It'll be ready when you get back, Mr. Brown," the cook quickly replied.

Brown smiled and headed off with Harvey.

ఞ

As the 19th century neared its end, the youthful town of Fort Macleod was rapidly moving beyond the rough military character that had shaped its first years. The island on the Oldman River that had served as the initial site of the North-West Mounted Police post had been abandoned in favor of a more accessible mainland site on the south side of the river, one that was less susceptible to annual flooding. Still, it was some time before the town's main street was anything more than a lonely dirt road, suited only for the cayuses tied to its numerous hitching posts, flanked by a few forlorn structures that appeared incapable of offering much resistance to the ever-present strong wind.

In the early 1890s, the Calgary & Edmonton Railway made known its intentions to lay track to Fort Macleod. For westerners, no other development was met with anything even close to the enthusiasm that greeted news of a railway line, because it meant access to markets and for immigrants. To many, "railway" was a synonym for "progress." However, in the spirit of rapacious railway promoters, the owners of the Calgary & Edmonton Railway announced that their new station would be built on the north side of the river—not on the south side, where the town was located. A significant financial boon to railway promoters came from the funds raised by the sale and development of land surrounding their stations, and they therefore usually opted for unsettled locations. This decision potentially spelled doom for the burgeoning community as dreams of boom-time were replaced with nightmares of depopulation. But early westerners were nothing if not stubborn. Rather than accept its fate, Fort Macleod met rapaciousness with single-minded determination. They boycotted the new station and its surrounding businesses. The unbroken unity displayed by local residents spoke volumes about community spirit. Their perseverance paid off, and the small community north of Fort Macleod slowly choked on its own greed. When the Canadian Pacific Railway subsequently floated the idea of constructing a line from Lethbridge to the interior of British Columbia, the Dominion government inserted a clause into the agreement that guaranteed a station would be located at Fort Macleod. The CPR finally reached the town in 1897.

Bull train in Fort Macleod. Fort Macleod was the North-West Mounted Police outpost that overlooked the end of the "Whoop-Up Trail." For a quarter of a century, the "Whoop-Up Trail," which stretched from Fort Benton in Montana to Fort Whoop-Up, near present-day Lethbridge, Alberta, was the main artery into the western plains. Transport companies carried tons of freight to government installations, cattle ranches and Indian reserves via the trail. Not all that freight was legal. The trail was the preferred route for smugglers of whisky, but as goods crossed the border into Canada, they came under the jurisdiction of the North-West Mounted Police who, with effective policing, essentially put an end to the illegal whisky trade. When the town was incorporated in 1892, the appellation "Fort" was unceremoniously dropped by locals who wanted to confine the town's perceived wild, whoop-up image to the history books. Some years later, Macleod became a "Fort" once again.

Fort Macleod's attempts at respectability were apparent as high culture and civilized forms of recreation became the fare of the day. In the town of some 500 white residents, organized clubs erupted like mushrooms after a rain. The musically inclined Quintette Club, the North-West Mounted Police Dramatic and the Athenaeum Club for debaters were only a few of the organizations that appealed to those with more refined tastes. Sports had already emerged as a popular pastime and, because so many of the residents had recent English ancestry, cricket, polo and golf continued to enjoy considerable popularity.

For those whose tastes were drawn to lower forms of culture, Fort Macleod proved just as attractive. Prostitution flourished, as it did throughout much of the West. Residents were able to brag that technically their community was free of the profession because most of the ladies plied their trade in establishments outside the town limits. On the supply side, most active were Native women. The more morally upright, or uptight, depending on one's perspective, regularly voiced concerns that nothing less than a slave trade was in operation. Accusations were vigorously flung, alleging that white men went to the reserves and purchased women, who they then forced into "the trade." In defense of the community's honor, it was quickly pointed out that, while this practice might well exist, the particular Native women in question had been prostitutes long before being sold into slavery.

Other recreations were to be found in the shot glass and the card deck—or some other form of gambling. While some businesses were more suspect than others, there was no shortage of watering holes where money flowed as freely as the booze. Potential patrons could choose from a variety of saloons, pool halls and licensed bars in hotels.

While Brown enjoyed the solitary life of the frontiersman, responding to the occasional tug of town life also
proved attractive. Whether for business or pleasure, a trip to
town went far towards addressing both his needs and his
wants. Upon arriving in Fort Macleod, Brown's likely practice was to address business matters first. His furs were taken
care of by the local Hudson's Bay Company post, which
was run by John Black. If Brown didn't get his supplies
there, then Smith & Brothers Wholesalers & Retailers could
supply all the goods required by a man living in the bush.
G.S. Stafford and Company, specializing in guns and ammunition, was also a likely stop; a man in Brown's line of work
could not afford to be without the tools of his trade. His
business completed, a meal at Bixby's or Bonton's restaurant
was a fitting conclusion to his transactions.

With time on his hands, Brown was next able to partake
of the town's goings-on. He doesn't seem to have been one
for participating in organized sports, but it's not a stretch to
imagine him as a bemused onlooker at a polo match, gently
shaking his head as he watched grown men on horseback
romp around the countryside in an effort to smash a small
ball with a mallet. Perhaps, at most, there was grudging
recognition of the players' horsemanship. Whether he could
grasp the local obsession with golf is unlikely. To a man
who used his guile to wrest a living from nature, seeing
folks who appeared to suffer from St. Vitus' Dance madly
contort themselves into unseemly positions in an effort to
strike a tiny white ball surely proved beyond serious con-
templation. And, to boot, they then followed the ball
around in the fashion of an obedient dog!

Brown was much more enthusiastic when he heard
news of upcoming events that appealed to his intellect. He
would read posters advertising such gatherings with great
interest.

Debate of The Young Peoples' Literary Society. Resolution of concern: There is more pleasure in anticipation than realization. First Thursday of the month. Meeting to be held at the Methodist Church. Refreshments to be served. All are welcome.

Activities of this type proved magnetic for Brown, and it is not difficult to imagine him seated in the audience, completely enjoying the intellectual milieu. It wasn't so much that Brown sought to improve himself; it was more that he saw man's intellectual abilities as a key component of his entire being. To let the intellect suffer and atrophy was an unconscionable failure in one's efforts to realize one's potential as a complete human being.

Brown's imbibing went beyond intellectual matters, of course, and he sought activities that took the edge off the physical sharpness of his way of life. He enjoyed a drink, and there were plenty of places in town where he could quench his thirst. Formally, whoop-up days were gone, but old habits die hard. Into the mid-1890s, drunkenness and its attendant behavior disturbed some, especially prohibition-minded Protestants. They saw such practices as deeply embarrassing to the community. The Macleod House (and later Hotel) was likely a favorite target of prohibitionists—and a favorite destination of Brown's. The Macleod House advertised that its bar served every type of liquid except water. It also demanded that its patrons be up by 6 AM so that the bedsheets could be used as tablecloths. It was the kind of no-nonsense place that would have appealed to the earthy Brown.

In the late 19th century, poolrooms challenged bars as the most wicked dens of iniquity because they combined two of the more destructive vices, gambling *and* drinking. In 1912, the forces of moral purity were successful in passing the *Pool*

Room Act, which required character checks on potential owners and regular inspection of their establishments, in a feeble effort to ensure there was no swearing or off-color stories told on the premises. Limitations on gambling were not successfully implemented in Brown's lifetime. Until the *Pool Room Act* was passed (and, truth be told, even after), those so inclined could enjoy unfettered freedom in La Chapelle's or Lester's Billiard Rooms and Shooting Gallery.

Brown probably also took time to visit the local race track. These establishments dotted the countryside, their popularity unmatched. Before World War I, horse racing was not only the sport of kings, it was the king of sports in Alberta. The race track combined two of Brown's favorite pastimes, horses and gambling. Because he had a well-trained eye for the former, it's likely he didn't suffer too much with the latter.

Brown undoubtedly enjoyed the occasional visit to the world of fleshly pleasures; suggestions to that effect certainly abound. Brown would have found little common ground with social reformers on the issue of prostitution—or on that of drinking, for that matter. His morality was of a different sort than that promulgated by the promoters of temperance and decency. Brown was guided by a personal relationship with nature, by an individualism often at odds with social mores. It would be surprising, indeed, to discover that he had not had first-hand familiarity with Fort Macleod's red light district. After all, the intellect was not the only component of a person's entire being. In the eyes of a man who lived life to the fullest, it would have been equally tragic to see those other parts atrophy.

ର୍ବଞ

Dusk was falling, and a man lurked in the shadows across the street from the town post office. He leaned on the whitewashed wall of the saloon with his wide-brimmed hat sloped low on his forehead and his hands in his pockets. If a passerby were to glance in his direction, he would have noticed that the man chewed gently on the ends of his flowing moustache. It was a habit acquired long ago. The man's attention was focused on a Mountie who stood next to a crate that rested outside the post office door. It appeared to the observer that the Mountie was standing guard over the crate, which was evidently a matter of some concern. The crate belonged to the man with the moustache, and although the box was labeled "Holy Bibles," it was full of smuggled whisky. The man in the shadows was, of course, Kootenai Brown. As he reflected on the situation, Brown realized that his retrieval of the crate was going to require something more than the usual pick-up.

Smuggling illegal whisky was still something of a going concern in the Canadian West even in the 1890s, even with the presence of the Mounties. To ensure that the West continued to run dry, the territorial government passed an order-in-council that allowed anyone to confiscate and destroy booze, and to arrest any person caught with booze in his or her possession. While the wording of this directive changed over time, its spirit generally remained the same. In later years, importation was legal if one secured a permit from the lieutenant-governor, a process so convoluted that only a career bureaucrat could have imagined navigating it. Permits were granted only to individuals for personal consumption, and sale of liquor for public consumption was prohibited.

A dry country, however, seemed to increase men's thirst. Laws were regularly, and fairly easily, circumvented. The largest loophole was the regulation that linked the permit to the bottle rather than to the drinker. Men brought both permit and bottle to their favorite watering hole. When the bottle ran dry, it was an easy matter for the person behind the bar to refill it with smuggled whisky. No one was the wiser. Ironically, given their mandate, the Mounties also contributed to the problem. Booze was pretty much an all-consuming preoccupation with the men in scarlet. Officially, much of their time was spent tracking whisky smugglers or rounding up town drunks. Unofficially, the scarlet was somewhat faded because a Mountie was just as likely to get sauced as any other man with a tickle in his throat. Unless an alcohol offence was serious, sober law enforcers tended to look the other way.

Even so, smuggling booze from the U.S. was considered a serious crime, and the Mounties drew a hard line at the border. American whisky peddlers broke Canadian law with impunity and undermined the loose liquor system that was in place. The Americans also caused havoc with the Natives. Much of the illegal booze found in southern Alberta flowed up from the States via the Benton Trail. So much booze flowed north to the Whoop-Up country above the border that to suggest the Benton Trail was better described as a river was no exaggeration. Indeed, despite laws and police, the demand remained, and there was ample opportunity to turn a profit selling smuggled hooch for those so inclined.

Like that of many frontier men, Brown's income was always spotty and he did what he had to do in order to earn a buck. Brown's participation in whisky smuggling was no doubt made easier by his old contacts from his days in Montana. In addition, Fort Benton had a strong Irish contingent, and many were experienced with the Whoop-Up country liquor trade. Given his own nationality, Brown could easily plug into this network.

But smuggling wasn't all about filling the coffers. It was the devious and humorous streak in Brown that drew him to smuggling. Sure, there was money to be made in it, and it was good to have an unlimited supply of booze at hand, but the fun of pulling the wool over the eyes of the authorities really made it all worthwhile. Part of the challenge lay in the past successes he had enjoyed. Over the years, Brown had smuggled the equivalent of a small distillery into Alberta. The Mounties were surely suspicious and, although they had never been able to catch him in the act, they were always on the lookout. This surveillance required Brown to employ a certain creativity as he plied his trade.

Shipping booze disguised as Bibles was a new approach for Kootenai Brown. He had figured that the authorities might be less suspicious of religious goods. As he looked at the Mountie, he realized he'd been mistaken in that assumption. The crate proved to be a red flag, and the authorities were obviously waiting to arrest the man who picked it up. Brown continued to study the Mountie. He was a young fellow, likely green to this line of work. A smile broke across Brown's face as a plan formed in his mind. He stepped out of the shadows and headed to the saloon, where he made some inquiries. Finally calling it a night, he made his way back to his room at the hotel to get a good night's sleep. He would be up with the birds to put his plan in action.

In the pre-dawn hour, the street was quiet and deserted save for the Mountie, who sat on a bench. He shook his head as he fought to fend off drowsiness.

"Sun'll be up soon and I'll be spelt off," he mumbled to himself. "I c'n make it."

The Mountie looked up, and what he saw almost made him fall off his perch. Out of the dark strode a figure in black. The long robe the figure wore hid its feet and caused it to resemble an otherworldly apparition, floating eerily across the street toward the post office. The Mountie quickly made the sign of the cross.

"Good morning, young man." The apparition spoke!

Somewhat relieved, the Mountie exhaled the air that had frozen in his chest. "Sacre bleu!" he exclaimed. "You damn near give me a 'eart attack." The figure came closer and the Mountie was able to make out a white collar around its neck. "Oh, forgive me Fat'er," he blurted in an attempt to make amends. "As I saw you makin' yer way across the street, I 'alf expected you to be carryin' a scythe. You scared the daylights out of me! As I swear on all the saints, I damn near 'ad a 'eart attack."

"There's an irony there, my son," Brown laughed, affecting a French accent to help complete his disguise. "I'm not quite the devil, glad to say. What is your name?"

"Constable Trudeau, Fat'er," the Mountie replied.

"You are young to be a Mountie, no?"

"I've been on the job fer only a week, Fat'er," he answered. "Not long since I left St. Maurice, in Quebec. The farmin' life wasn't fer me."

"Indeed," Brown replied, smiling. "You and me both." Brown extended his hand. "Constable Trudeau, I'm Father Lacombe. Glad to make your acquaintance."

"Fat'er Lacombe!" exclaimed the young man. "It is indeed an honor to meet the man who is a legend in all Quebec. Do you know that it was the inspiration provided by yer stories that encouraged me to come out west? My younger brudder, Pierre, entered the priesthood because of you, Fat'er Lacombe." They were quiet for a moment while the Mountie looked at Brown. "You know, if you don't mind me sayin', you don't look at all like I've 'eard you described. 'Ow could anyone fail to mention that moustache and long 'air?"

"Recent additions, my child," Brown explained. "But on to the matter at hand. I've been awaiting a shipment of Bibles for use in my mission. They were to arrive yesterday. Today I leave for the Blackfoot reserve up north and I had hoped to leave early. I had even hoped that you could give me access to my goods."

"I guess this is yer crate 'ere, Fat'er," replied the Mountie, pointing to the box. "But there's a problem."

"What problem?" asked Brown.

"Well..." the Mountie hesitated.

"Out with it, boy," Brown commanded.

"Fat'er, I've been instructed to watch this crate and to arrest the man who comes to retrieve it," the young constable said.

"Yes, well, I suppose that would explain your presence. But it seems odd that you would want to arrest the owner of a crate of Bibles, no?" Brown asked.

"The feelin' of my superior is that this is not a box of Bibles, but contraband whisky," the Mountie said, his voice falling off with each word.

"Preposterous!" Brown exclaimed. "Such a deception would be sacrilegious! The perpetrator would surely endure the fires of hell."

"I've 'eard there are men who would take that chance," offered the Mountie.

"Humph! Chance plays no part in God's punishment, young man. I certainly hope that you do not take me for one of those men, my son."

"Oh no, Fat'er. Certainly not."

"Then I may take my Bibles?"

The Mountie hesitated. "Fat'er, I've got orders from my superior. I can't let this crate go."

Brown's voice rose in the pre-dawn light. "You question my integrity! Such an action surely puts your immortal soul at peril. Tongues of fire will dance over your flesh for an eternity! As the flesh melts, you will beg for mercy. But the begging will fall on deaf ears, for the Lord does not look kindly on those who question his humble messengers."

"No, no—you misunderstand me, Fat'er," the trembling Mountie pleaded. "Don't even suggest such a t'ing. I'm certain that if my superior knew it was the great Fat'er Lacombe who was the receiver of this crate, my presence 'ere would not 'ave been required. Can you wait until the sergeant comes?"

"Son, the Lord's work does not observe man's schedules, nor does it abide unnecessary delays. It is imperative that I go north. Crowfoot waits for me," Brown added for good measure. "At this meeting the great chief will make his decision on conversion, and should he convert, many of his red brothers will follow." Brown made the sign of the cross. "You do not want to be the man who stands as an obstacle to the saving of so many souls."

"Take it! Take the crate, Fat'er, and Godspeed," said the Mountie, waving his hands at the box.

"Thank you, son. You are a monument to your faith." Brown bent over and popped the cover off the crate. He pulled a Bible from the top. "Take this Bible, and tonight, before you rest, read John, chapter two. Perhaps it will bring better understanding to one so young."

"T'ank you, Fat'er," replied the young Mountie, much relieved at the sight of the Bibles. "I will. May God go wit' you on yer mission," he called as Brown hurried down the street, carrying his crate.

"Who knows, my child," Brown called over his shoulder. "God's ways are mysterious. But one thing we know for certain is that He helps those who help themselves."

The Mountie continued to sit on the bench, his Bible clutched tightly in his hands. Slowly, the sun's rays gave a new life to the town, and before long townsfolk spilled onto the street. The young constable decided to read the passage suggested by Father Lacombe. He opened his new possession in anticipation of the wisdom that awaited. In John, chapter two, he read the story of Jesus at the wedding at Cana, where the Lord transformed water...into wine.

The light of revelation indeed fell on the Mountie. He darted off in the direction that the imposter had taken. On the way, he passed a local church and noticed a small stack of Bibles on its steps. He scanned the trail that led out of town.

"Damn," he muttered. With stooped shoulders he returned to town, aware that he would soon be the laughingstock of the entire force. And that was if he was still a member!

Meanwhile, the man he sought had taken an obscure route west, his load lightened by a thoughtful contribution of Bibles to the local congregation—Bibles that had concealed the large supply of whisky that rested underneath.

CRISIS AND CONTENTMENT
IN THE LATE 1890S

KOOTENAI BROWN stood on the shore of Middle Kootenay
Lake. Although it was late spring, the breeze from across the
water still had a bite to it. Brown's eyes were drawn sky-
ward, and they fell upon Bear's Hump. It was an odd rock
formation, something halfway between a hill and a mountain, protruding in a curved and distended fashion from a
larger adjacent peak. For anyone who'd seen a grizzly, the
resemblance between the outcropping and the hump that
rose above the sandy beast's shoulders was striking. A few
scattered reddish jack pine and green fir fought to give the
otherwise gray rock face some color. Brown decided to
make his way to the top.

It was about a kilometer to the summit, and although
the climb was steep, Brown enjoyed the short hike. It gave
him a chance to stretch his legs. The songs of warblers and
kinglets kept time, and he even flushed out a couple of
blue grouse. A man in the bush never turns down a meal,
so Brown slipped out his Colt .45 and brought down both
grouse with two clean shots. It was hardly a challenge.

He strung them up in a tree so he could retrieve them on his descent. After a leisurely half-hour, he found himself on the peak.

The crisp breeze that had refreshed below was transformed above into a cold wind. Brown removed his wide-brimmed hat and let the wind blow through his hair. The sweat on his brow quickly evaporated. He breathed deeply and surveyed the scene that lay before him. He stood at the point of a right angle that gave a clear view of Middle Kootenay Lake extending to the east and Upper Kootenay Lake stretching to the south. Majestic mountains on all sides framed the clear blue waters that gently rippled in the wind. Peaks and crevices were white with the last of winter's snow and glistened like gems in the rays of the westerly sun. The view possessed a beauty that transcended words. It was a vista that moved a man, and it touched Brown deeply. Nature had that effect on him.

But he was still a man, and as he took in what lay before him, Brown could hardly be blamed if selfish thoughts slipped into his mind. With little false grandeur, he could claim that this was his land. It wasn't something he'd say to anyone else, but there was little self-delusion in the thought that he was pretty much king of what he surveyed. It was the late 1890s, and there wasn't even a handful of settlers living anywhere near the place. Brown wanted to keep it that way, as pristine as possible. Too many newcomers— be they settlers intent on bringing new shape to the land, or businessmen determined to plunder the wealth of local resources—would be a tragic disservice to the region. More than that, it would wound Brown. His kingdom would be tainted, and the nourishment it provided would dissipate. The link he felt with it would be severed.

The selfishness that colored Brown's attitude was to change over the last couple of decades of his life. He never

On the border between Canada and the United States in Alberta, Waterton Lakes National Park (originally Kootenay Lakes Forest Reserve) was the brainchild of John George (Kootenai) Brown. He fought to preserve its unique landscape of flat, dry prairies leading to soaring mountains and jewel-like lakes and its variety of plant and animal life. He lobbied for the preservation of this area for many years and finally was rewarded for his efforts in 1895 when the Canadian government established the forest reserve. The park underwent changes in size over the years and it now encompasses 525 km^2. In 1932 Waterton Lakes National Park joined with Montana's Glacier National Park to create the first international peace park.

wavered in his efforts to have more of the region protected, but his motives shifted. He became less interested in ensuring that the Kootenay Lakes area remained untouched for his own benefit; he came to feel that was a malignant disposition. He came to appreciate that anyone could—and should—enjoy that which touched him so deeply. Their enjoyment would not diminish his sustenance. In fact, the pleasure that others took from the region intensified the meaning of the place for him. Still, the transition was not an easy one. To make the shift, Brown had to learn more about himself and find a deeper self-awareness that came only after crisis. After some soul-searching, Brown came to understand these truths, and with that understanding he chose to dedicate his remaining years to enhancing the experience of those who visited the area.

෨෨

"He did what?!" asked Marie Rose.

"He kick me out," wept Isabella. "Kootenai, he kick me out. Don't need me, he say."

Marie Rose placed her pail of chicken feed on the ground, stepped out from behind the chicken-wire fence and put her arm around the shoulder of her distraught friend. Between sobs, the whole story slipped out.

Over the past few months Brown had taken to inviting a pair of sisters from Fort Macleod to the Brown homestead. For the most part, Brown guided the women on day trips. It was hardly unusual; the Brown residence often had visitors who sought to follow someone as prominent as Brown through uncertain mountain passes. Isabella, a trusting wife, never suspected anything was amiss. A dutiful wife, she would pack lunches for the trio before they set out on their daily excursions and have meals prepared for them upon their return. She did, however, think her exclusion a little odd, as she had long been Brown's regular companion when he guided parties. Her camp skills had always been welcome. Her suggestion that she might accompany her husband on a trip with the two sisters was greeted by a firm "no" from her husband.

Matters deteriorated from there. The company of the two women took on a more permanent character. Their presence in the small, two-room cabin was bad enough, but in addition, the two never lifted a finger to help Isabella. After they had lived at the house for a number of weeks, Isabella finally had enough and, in her reserved fashion, spoke her mind.

"Kootenai, these girls no good. They go, or I go," she stated flatly.

Brown flew into a rage. "Who do you think you are?" he shouted. "You overestimate your value! You are free to go. They will stay in your place, and they'll have no trouble filling your moccasins," he scoffed. "And the milk won't turn sour if *they* look at it!"

Isabella stayed the night, but she got no rest. The next morning, she packed her few belongings and rode to Marie Rose Smith's place in Pincher Creek. Marie Rose was a long-time friend of the Browns and they regularly called on one another. It was a hard ride, nearly 60 kilometers, and the steady stream of tears that blurred Isabella's vision made the journey more difficult. All that she had done for him! The well-tended campfires, the steaming meals on the table when he came through the door, her companionship on so many lonely nights—all of it was meaningless. When she reached Rose Marie's house, Isabella was exhausted.

"Never you mind, Isabella," consoled Marie Rose. "You're married to him, and that's your house just as much as his. The man's got a temper like a hot oven, and it's best just to give him some time to cool down. It won't be long before he'll come to his senses. And you know that you're welcome to stay here for as long as that takes."

Isabella nodded gratefully and brought her few belongings into the house. The next few days were difficult ones. Isabella poured out her heart to Marie Rose. It was all "Kootenai this" and "Brown that." Marie Rose came to understand how deeply Isabella loved her husband.

"Oh, Marie Rose, that man make me laugh. I 'member when we stop at Henry's halfway house one time. We was in our buggy and Kootenai had drunk two gallon of whisky. That man love his drink. He like to say, 'Let's have 'nudder drink an' dream some more.' "

She paused to sniffle. "At Henry's, he step out of the buggy, but miss the step and land smack on the groun'. He got stuck between the wheel and the box. He speak such words! He jus' like a squirrel who can't crack a nut when he mad. I not un'erstan' all, but Mr. Upton was there wit' his wife an' daughters, and he say that Kootenai's words were not very nice in front of them Upton girls. All this time our dogs, Spotty and Small Dog, were runnin' roun' barkin' like crazy. Kootenai had to move the horses to get free. Then the wheel run over his foot. Oh, did he curse those beasts!" she laughed.

"And he loved the jokes," Isabella continued. "Once I was so sick, I need a doctor from Macleod. Kootenai rush to get him, but it took t'ree days. By then I well. But Kootenai play trick on doctor. He say, 'Doc, it woun't be right for you to come all this way wit'out us givin' you somet'ing in return. How about joinin' us for meal?' Doctor liked the idea of travelin' on a full belly, so he agree," she said.

"While we eat, Kootenai talk of usin' poison to kill animals. He ask, 'Doc, is it okay to eat poisoned game?' Doc say, 'Only if you wanna end up as dead as the animal.' Well, Kootenai get real serious. 'Doc,' he say, 'you best prepare to meet your maker. The bear that we eatin' was poisoned by me near Sofa Mountain.' "

She continued, "The doctor start to choke. He spit out food from his mout' so fast! His face so red—he don't look like no doctor! 'Good God, man!' he shout. 'Wha' have you done?' Kootenai tell him to relax. 'Me and Nichemoos have eaten poison meat lots before,' he say. 'You just got to cut out its guts before the poison spread.' He right too. The doctor still not happy, though. He leave and not say goo'bye. Kootenai shout to him, 'Careful, Doc, you don't know wha' mischief you find on the trail!' " She and Marie Rose shared a laugh.

"Kootenai could be serious, too," continued Isabella. "Many times he tell me of his visions. He say that someday machines fly t'rough the mountains like great eagles. When he die, he tell me to watch for coyote, 'cause it will be him. Kootenai use many words I not un'erstan', but I listen as he talk. I wish I could hear him now," she said, beginning to cry again.

"Put your mind off it, Isabella," advised Marie Rose. "You've had nothing but tea for days. You really must eat."

"Is good, but I not hungry. I stay too long. Tomorrow I go see Mrs. Scheers in the fort."

"Nonsense. You know you are welcome to stay as long as you want."

"I know."

Still, the next day Isabella made her way into Fort Macleod. In her mind she had already made plans to move north to be with relatives in Hobbema, near Edmonton.

Brown, meanwhile, was enjoying his new companions. Cameron Lake was but a short hike from the cabin. Red Rock Canyon was also an attractive setting for those who

allowed nature to touch their souls. The trail that led to it
provided a stark and compact example of the contrasts that
define so much of the region; rolling brown prairies quickly
gave way to towering mountains. Over the eons, a small
stream had carved out the canyon, and though it was dominated by reddish rocks, hints of green and gray were visible
when the sun's rays shone just so. It takes very little imagination to see Brown and his companions seated deep in the
gorge, the women listening to Brown recite poetry, tell of
his past adventures or sing in his melodic voice. As often as
not, the words he spoke came from his own romantic heart.
It was not only the flow of warm, honey-like words that
made Brown attractive to the opposite sex. He was a good-
looking man, one of those whose appearance improved
with age. He was an appealing sight to quite a few women
other than the two sisters.

Like Adam, Brown was to lose his paradise. News of
Isabella's departure spread quickly through Fort Macleod.
One of those who heard of her flight was the sisters'
brother. He didn't take kindly to the revelation, and he
was soon on horseback to retrieve his siblings. The ladies
returned willingly; perhaps they discovered that, without a
servant, homesteading was too much like work. Brown
was forced to reconsider his circumstances. His thoughts
fell easily to his Nichemoos. Sure, she had not provided
much in the way of intellectual companionship. She was a
simple woman, not the thinker that Brown was. But
through the years, her value as a wife had manifested in
many other ways. She was an asset on the trail. She could
clean game and either cook it or prepare the hides with
equal ability. He thought of the laughs they had shared;
she wasn't one given to regular chuckling, but when
something tickled her funny bone she laughed long and
hard. It was infectious. She did not have Olivia's beauty,

Women of his day might have considered Brown to be a good-looking man, even though in his younger days he had a hound-dog look. His big, drooping moustache almost made it appear as if there were no chin beneath his fleshy cheeks and floppy slouch hat. But years of hard frontier living had toughened him up so the lean, rugged features of his cheeks and chin were more prominent. The long hair remained, but the moustache was more carefully trimmed and both had turned a distinguished silver. Dressed in his Stetson, sloped gently to the right, a buckskin jacket and, on occasion, his angora chaps, the man cut a figure. He may not appeal to the modern woman, but in his day, his rugged looks and adventuring nature would have been appealing to a goodly number of the female population.

but Brown had come to accept that there was a place in his heart, once filled with love for his first wife, that would remain forever empty. Ultimately, Brown realized that he had other needs and, despite himself, concluded that he depended on his second wife.

"Maybe there's love in that," he mumbled to himself. Brown set out to get his Nichemoos back.

After inquiries, Brown discovered that she was still in Fort Macleod. He rode directly to Mrs. Scheers' house. When he entered the dwelling, his eyes fell upon his wife, lost in the bluish-gray haze from the smoke of the pipe on which she chewed.

"Nichemoos, please come back with me," Brown said.

"Go 'way. I'm no match for your white girls in silks and powders," she replied. "I not good 'nough."

"Nonsense! I admit that I have made mistakes and I have said bad things…but they are behind us now. Please join me back at the cabin," he pleaded.

"No."

Brown was stumped. Isabella was being too stubborn about this. It would take a more persuasive approach. "Nichemoos, please come. I will get you a gallon of whisky."

"No."

Damnation, Brown thought to himself. *She is awfully fond of the drink, and to turn it down…well, she must be* very *upset.*

Beaten, Brown left, hands in pocket, head held low. He didn't give up, though. Over the following days, he was Isabella's constant companion, coaxing her, using his considerable skill to try to win her back. His attempts at charm were matched—easily—by her reticence. Brown decided that he could only have success with the assistance of Mrs. Scheers.

"Mrs. Scheers," Brown pleaded, "I am at my wits' end. Please help me to win back my Nichemoos." Brown hesitated. "I will give you $10 to do so."

Mrs. Scheers could see the desperation in Brown's eyes, and could imagine a new bonnet to cover her own eyes, so she agreed to do what she could.

"Tell Isabella that I will give her some horses and a bill of sale in her name. Tell her I know that what I did was wrong and that I'll never do it again."

Brown came by the house later that night to see if his new strategy was successful.

"Well, Mrs. Scheers?" he asked expectantly.

"All is fine," she replied. "Mrs. Brown has agreed to return with you."

"Ahhh," sighed Brown in great relief.

Brown's adventure had cost him. Mrs. Scheers had $10 in her pocket, and his wife had a bunch of fine horses and a wagon full of grub. Brown had also discovered something important. Up to this point he had lived a carefree life, thinking of little but himself. It wasn't good enough. Now that he knew how important another was to him, he was determined to change.

ॐ

Brown looked up from his cup of tea. His eyes followed the rising steam as it drifted toward the ceiling of his cabin and he blew at it. The mist from his own breath caught the steam and it tumbled toward the edge of the table before once again beginning their ascent.

"I do declare, Nichemoos," he said finally, "this is one hell of a cold morning! Just look at the damn frost on the window."

Brown unwrapped his hands from the warm cup and made his way to the window. He scratched at it with his fingernail.

"Must be quarter of an inch thick," he muttered. "We'll have to get some coal in for the winter. If the rest of it's anything like December was, we're in for a real cold one."

"Coal'll be real good," replied Isabella. It meant she wouldn't have to get up through the night to stoke the fire.

Brown continued to scrape away at the window. Eventually he could see the blurred scene outside. Suddenly he began to rub the ice-free space quickly with the sleeve of his shirt.

"I'll be damned! Is that an antelope across the lake?!"

He made for the door and threw it open.

"By God, it is!"

This was a real treat. Save the occasional rabbit, which only made for decent stew, fresh meat in winter was a rare meal indeed. Brown put on his coat and pulled on his mukluks. He grabbed his rifle from where it stood near the door.

"Get your knife ready, Nichemoos," he thundered as he leapt through the doorway. "We'll be dining like royalty tonight!"

Isabella laughed and rubbed her hands together.

As Brown strode across the clearing to the water's edge, he stopped short when a voice called to him.

"Kootenai Brown, I hope you don't have your eyes on my antelope over yonder!"

Brown turned around.

"Jack Street, you old rascal! What brings you out here on this bloody cold day?"

"Parcel came into town for you. I felt like a ride in the crisp air," Street explained. "A couple of miles east of here, I picked up the trail of that fine buck over there."

"Let's divvy it up, then," Brown suggested.

Street dismounted and the pair began to walk across the ice on the narrow stretch of water to the far side of the lake where the antelope was standing. Suddenly Brown fell straight down. Within a split second, only his head and one hand, clutched desperately to the jagged edge of the hole in the ice, were visible.

"Damn it, Jack!" Brown cried. "I'm slipping! I can't hold on!"

Street moved quickly. He was flat on his belly, reaching toward Brown. He didn't want to get too close for fear of the ice cracking. If he joined Brown in the water, he'd be no help to either of them. The only thing he had to extend to his old friend was his rifle. "Grab hold of the barrel!" Street cried, his hands tight on its butt.

Brown lifted his hand out of the water and gripped the rifle. His wet leather mitten stuck to the cold metal and allowed him to hold tight. Slowly, Street began to edge backwards. It was demanding work, but soon Brown was able to kick free from the hole.

"Never thought I'd be so happy to see the business end of a Winchester!" Brown chattered.

Street laughed, pulled off his coat and wrapped it around his friend. They hurriedly made their way back to the cabin. Isabella had observed the near disaster and she already had the whisky poured. Brown stripped down and put on some warm clothes.

"I'll go get the supper," called Street as he went out the door. Brown didn't respond. He was too busy pouring a second helping from the gallon of hooch that was before him on the table.

Jack Street was one of Brown's few close friends. They had developed a strong partnership over the years, starting when Street was a Mountie. Once Street quit the force, the two entered into a partnership of sorts. Together, they guided parties into the backcountry. Other times, just the two of them disappeared, often for weeks on end. It was hard to find any two men who knew the country better, or two men who were closer. Their partnership went beyond business; they were like family.

Truth be told, Street's energy too often let Brown's laziness surface. Street was an excellent shot, and he had little trouble keeping the pot full when in the backwoods. He was a more careful guide than Brown, and he more willingly assisted sportsmen in bringing their trophies down from the mountains. When the men were so employed, Isabella usually accompanied them. Her skills at cleaning and cooking game were unmatched, and she never let a campfire burn out. For the most part, Brown was able to enjoy telling his stories, hunting for big game and being in the outdoors. There were no complaints because all three were content with their roles.

Not long after the incident that saw Brown nearly drown, the two men were hired as guides for a party of hunters out of Fort Macleod. Brown and Street had built their reputation on being able to find animals in any season, so they always took care to be aware of where there might be game. Rare was the sportsman who returned home without a story to tell and wild meat for dinner. As spring approached, the men had scouted out some moose and bighorn sheep in the southern portion of the region, near the United States border. The trio of hunters made their way to Brown's cabin, where the two guides joined them.

"Boys, I hope you brought the elephant rifles," said Brown. "I got a feeling we're going to see some big game! And from the looks of it, there's plenty of it to go around— so I hope you brought lots of ammo, too!"

There was little better way of starting off a hunting trip than with such words of encouragement, and as Brown loaded up the packhorses, the hunters were bubbling with excitement. The sun hadn't reached its noon zenith before the men were on their way.

The snow had melted considerably over the past couple of weeks, and while open patches of ground were few, the depth of what was left of the white stuff was insignificant. The traveling was easy, and the horses hardly broke a sweat. They made their way along the Kootenay River, swinging west just beyond the upper reaches of the middle lake. The route would allow them to bypass the many small streams that feed the lake—no sense in taking any more chances with risky ice. It was a glorious day for such a journey. The cloudless sky seemed like it was a great inverted blue bowl. The snow glistened like an overflowing treasure chest as it caught the sun's rays. The winter birds were still around, joined by the earliest of spring's arrivals. The hunting party was treated to nature's symphony as they made their way.

They were soon in the shadow of Sheep Mountain, Brown's favorite hunting spot in the whole region.

"Boys, this here is Sheep Mountain, a hunter's paradise. In early summer and fall, you can sit on a bluff and chew on a piece of grass as you take your pick of beast. Brought down a grizzly here a couple of years back. Let me tell you, there's nothing to keep you warm on a cold Kootenay night like the hide of full-grown grizzly," Brown assured the others.

They soon reached their destination. "There she is, boys," said Street. "Mount Boswell—named after a fellow in the British Boundary Commission a few years back."

"Boswell, hell," grumbled Brown. He hated that European names were replacing the traditional Native names. He felt it took away from the history of the place. Still, he hadn't heard the Native name for this particular peak, so he let Street's pronouncement stand.

The men began to set up camp. The tents were up and a fire was nicely burning in no time at all. The sun was low in the sky.

"Boys, it's too late to hunt today, so we'll make a start of it tomorrow," said Brown as he settled in near the fire.

"I'm going to head over to the mountain and see if I can pick up any sign of game," said Street.

After the men were seated around the fire, Brown said, "I've about had my fill of coffee. Who's up for something a little stronger?" Soon the cups were brimming with whisky.

"You folks ever hear tell of a white buffalo?" asked Brown.

The men shook their heads in unison and settled in for one of Brown's stories. His storytelling was the stuff of legend, and it was a primary reason the men had chosen him to guide their hunt.

"I know you folks are new to this place," Brown began, "and it might sound unreal to you, but there was a time when you could stand on Lookout Butte, where the mountains meet the prairies, and see nothing but buffalo for miles. Though you knew it was there, you couldn't see the grass they stood on. Back in those days, it was mostly Indians and half-breeds that hunted the beasts. And there was damn little waste. They used every part of the animal, from tongue to hoof." He looked around at his enchanted audience.

"Wasn't long after that the professional hunters began their slaughter," he continued. "For the most part, they were after hides—and they left the carcasses to rot in the sun. There was also a bounty on the buffalo. The Americans actually paid men to cull the herds in great numbers because they felt that they couldn't rein in the Sioux until the buffalo were gone. I figure they were about right about that."

"You suppose the Yanks did the right thing?" asked one of the party.

"Don't get me wrong," replied Brown. "In the march of civilization, the buffalo had to go and so did the Indian. There is no place for their way of life in this new world. Still, it's a damn tragedy! For a long time, though, there were still plenty of buffalo around. Once I found myself out still-hunting, which means I didn't have my horse. The snow was on the ground and I had dug out a hollow to hide my presence. Not that the buffalo gave a damn about me—it was one of the few beasts that a hunter wouldn't scare off. Anyway, as I lay in the snow, a herd wandered close, about 500 yards away. Right smack in the middle was a white buffalo!" He stared into space, transfixed momentarily by the memory.

"I'll tell you, I was surprised! I'd seen white beaver and white muskrat before—hell, even a white deer—but never a white buffalo. It wasn't quite the color of the snow…a little creamier perhaps. But it was a full-grown bull. All I could think of was how nice that hide'd be in my cabin," he said.

"Problem was, there were about 30 or 40 buffalo between me and it. You can bet that I wasn't going to let that little detail stand in my way. In an effort to get a clear line of fire, I began shooting the beasts. I brought down 10 and was beginning to think that a clear shot was only moments away when something startled the herd. Off they went, headed south. I couldn't follow without my horse, and that was the last I saw of it." He looked around again.

"A few years later, I was down in Benton at the I.G. Baker store," Brown added. "Saw a couple of albino buffalo hides there. The trader there told me those were the only two he'd ever seen, and he'd had thousands of hides pass through his hands."

"See a price on them?" asked one of the men.

"Not for sale," Brown answered. "Though most everything else in Benton was. That was a depraved place of Old
Testament proportions. I had some troubles there, but, God,
there was a lot to love about the place! Before I tell you
about Benton, what say we recharge our mugs?"

There was quick and unanimous agreement on that
idea. Brown picked up the jug and began to generously fill
all cups. As he placed the jug back on the ground, he heard
a low rumble just within earshot. Suddenly, a rifle cracked.
Brown looked up, his eyes immediately drawn to the source
of the noise. He saw Jack Street, away in the distance, on the
side of Boswell Mountain. Street was waving his arms.
Seconds later he was swallowed by an avalanche rolling
down the side of the mountain.

Brown was off with a speed he had rarely demonstrated
even as a young man. The hunting party followed at a distance. When they arrived at the base of the mountain,
Brown was already digging wildly. They could all see that
the situation was hopeless, though the opinion went unspo-
ken. Instead, they joined Brown in his task. Under the full
moon they worked into the late hours of the night. Finally,
one of the men spoke the words no one wanted to hear.

"He's dead, Kootenai. No one could still be alive."

Brown collapsed on the snow. In a rare sign of emotion,
he let out a wail that pierced the night. Eventually he
joined the others and they slowly made their way back
to camp.

Brown returned to the mountain once more in the
spring, when the last of the snows had melted. Already, the
peak had become known as Street Mountain. There was no
sign of the body at its base. Brown began to climb and soon
stumbled upon a crevice that was barely visible from
ground level. Deep in its belly was the body of Jack Street.

There was no way to retrieve the corpse and even if there had been, Brown wasn't of a mind to move it. The spot came to serve as his friend's final resting place.

A lonely Kootenai Brown sat on the edge of the precipice, trying to make sense of it all. What nature gives, natures takes. Man, he figured, has little influence over either outcome. Although Brown still guided and hunted after this sorrowful event, neither activity brought the enjoyment it once had.

৯৯

On the heels of the Street tragedy, Brown made a significant decision. In the early summer of 1898, he formalized his spiritual journey by becoming a Full Fellow in the Theosophical Society. Ironically, one of the first to know of his decision was Reverend Middleton, a local Anglican clergyman and one of Brown's good friends.

Middleton emerged from the cool shelter of the trees and hit the wall of still air, sticky and hot, that had taken command of the open space that surrounded Brown's cabin. Even the bugs were inactive, having surrendered to the damp blanket that seemed to have been thrown across the clearing. Middleton examined what lay before him. The cabin was a simple structure, consisting of squared-off logs that had been plastered together with mud. It was nearly square, a little longer than it was wide. Brown had gone to the trouble of importing glass for windows, still an expensive proposition in those days, and the sun's rays were admitted through two openings on the south side of the building. In a feeble effort to dry laundry on the humid day, clothes were scattered on the bushes. A makeshift triangular rack had been constructed off to one side of the cabin, and thin strips of venison were hanging on it to dry. On another rack, a moose hide was pulled tight and Mrs. Brown was busy scraping it.

"Good day, Chee-pay-tha-qua-ka-soon," the minister called out in Cree.

"Hello, Mi'leton," Isabella replied, stopping in mid-stroke to address him. Middleton noticed the beads of sweat streaming down her face. He shook his head in a mixture of disbelief and a little pity at the terribly physical life of Native women.

"Will you be joining Brown and me on our trip to Chief Mountain?" the reverend inquired.

"No," she replied. "This hide mus' be prepared 'fore it dries out."

"You should have seen the moose, Middleton!" exclaimed Brown, as he strode from the cabin. His long hair flowed from beneath his wide-brimmed hat. Hot though it was, Brown had on his buckskin jacket, and the long fringes danced with each step he took. "A majestic old buck. Brought it down just over by Bear's Hump, not a mile from here. Stood five feet at the chest and had an enormous rack. I expect the meat'll be tough and gamey, though. No mind. Nichemoos works wonders with the pot."

Brown walked over to Middleton, and the two old friends shook hands. In many ways, theirs was an odd pairing. Middleton was the principal of a nearby residential school for Native children. Some years earlier, Brown had heard that the establishment was in the market for food and, because a frontiersman is always on the lookout for ready cash, he had made his way out to the school. The principal had little money to offer because residential schools were run on an unconscionably low budget provided by a parsimonious Dominion government. Brown, however, was not a man without feelings. The sight of the

Pictured here is a group of Anglican clergymen from southern Alberta around 1914 with Canon S.H. Middleton on the extreme left. He and Brown were great friends and had many philosophical discussions during their times together. These metaphysical discussions with the reverend may have interested Brown, but he had his own ideas about spirituality so, in later years, he joined the Theosophical Society. The Society expounded an organic spiritual understanding, emphasizing the unity of matter and spirit, and the sacredness of natural cycles in life. For the Theosophists, there was an indication of divinity in everything in the natural world.

students surely reminded him of his own children, and he parted with his meat for a price well below market value. Other donations had followed. Through small talk, the men soon found they shared an interest in intellectual topics. Brown finally suggested that they take a trip together into the mountains. He suggested to Middleton that nature's surroundings stimulated philosophical discussion. Middleton agreed to the outing and discovered how right Brown was. Since that first trip, the duo had regularly packed into the backcountry.

"Ready to head out?" asked Middleton.

"Just about," Brown replied.

Brown threw a few supplies on a packhorse, then saddled up his own buckskin. He went over and kissed Isabella on the cheek, a rare sign of affection, but Middleton knew of the very real bond that had come to link the two. Brown whistled to his dog, Spotty, and the men were soon deep in the forest on a trail that headed east. At first, the pair were silent, preferring to let their senses fill as they made their way through the trees. Their eyes feasted on summer's banquet of color, so evident in yellow buttercups, white orchids, red paintbrush and other striking plants.

Brown was the first to break the silence. "I believe that there might just be something to this theory of evolution," he offered. The practice of the two men was to decide on some text to discuss on their journey. Darwin's *On the Origin of Species*, published a few decades before, remained as topical as ever and held some interest for both men. In anticipation of their backwoods trip, they had both read it. "It makes plain sense that we're moving to a higher state of affairs."

"I can't disagree with that," Middleton replied thoughtfully. "It seems to me, however, that the question is whether such movement is the result of nature's cruel forces or God's compassionate hand."

"I'm not so certain that there's such a great difference between the two," countered Brown. "I've spent many a day riding the trail and just as many nights under the stars. It doesn't seem to me that God's majesty can be any greater than what I've seen in nature. Perhaps they're the same."

As Brown spoke, the trail wove onto the crest of a bluff overlooking Sofa Creek, its many ripples highlighted in rainbow hues by the unobstructed rays of the sun. An unknown force held the men in thrall and they silently drank in the view. A lone eagle floated lazily above.

"Middleton, I do believe that when my body can no longer take the weight of this world and shakes off these mortal coils, my spirit will take another form," Brown confided. "I can only hope it's that of a wild creature—an eagle, or perhaps a coyote."

"I think there's likely a greater destination than that in store for us, Brown," Middleton replied. "I agree, there is an indescribable beauty in what lies before us. Nevertheless, I know deep in my heart that its Creator has prepared a place for us that this world, even at its best, can offer only a pale comparison."

"What I know in my heart is based on what I see," said Brown. "After years of experience, and a great deal of thought, I can no longer take on faith what might be."

"It's indeed interesting how the thoughts and experiences of one man can lead to a totally different conclusion than those of another," replied Middleton, who had long since come to regard Brown as an intellectual soul mate rather than a potential convert. "I hope we are both pleased with our destination."

They continued on. Along the way, their presence interrupted the peaceful routine of a couple of grouse. Brown

brought them down with two quick shots of his rifle and
tossed them onto his packhorse. They soon passed a small
river, and Chief Mountain became prominent. Glowing red
in the sunset, the bare rock dwarfed its surroundings. It was
a unique geological formation; years of erosion had effectively separated the tower from the adjacent mountain
range. When the two men made camp for the night, they
dined like kings, truly believing that royalty had it little better. Satiated, the men wound up the evening with smokes
and coffee, nestled in the mountain's shelter, under the halo
of a full moon.

"Brown, you're right—this *is* a heavenly place!"
Middleton exclaimed.

"Not only beautiful, but mystical," Brown replied. "The
Kootenay and Blackfoot consider this place to be sacred.
Many an Indian has come here on a vision quest. They
would wait here for days, alone, until the spirit world
made a connection. The overture came in the form of an
animal, which offered its protection. A powerful animal
might offer its special abilities to the one on the quest. I've
heard tell of those who were granted the power to see
into the future, or to cure a man who was near death's
door. Most times, though, the animal came to act as a
guardian spirit."

"We could all use one of those," suggested Middleton.

"I come here myself to do some soul-searching from
time to time," Brown admitted. "I can't say that I ever
went on a vision quest. That way isn't my way. But the
past year has seen some difficult times, and I needed to
sort things out. Didn't seem to be a better place to do that
than right here."

Middleton knew something of the challenges Brown
had recently endured. His good hunting companion, Jack
Street, had been killed before Brown's eyes. Middleton

Chief Mountain is a striking landmark in the international peace park created by the joining of Waterton Lakes National Park, Alberta, and Glacier National Park, Montana. On a clear day it can be seen from Calgary, 267 kilometers (160 miles) north. The mountain is known as *Ninastakis* in Blackfoot, and because this spiritual site dominates the landscape of the area it has been endowed with origin-myth significance—it was there that three tribes were created. Place names were often given at the sentimental, patriotic or geological whimsy of settlers and explorers of a particular region. It is not clear how Chief Mountain acquired its name, but at some point in time the Waterton Lakes, also known as Kootenay Lakes, were also named for this mountain. The name Chief Mountain Lakes appears on several maps of the region including one that was with the Palliser Report of 1860.

could only imagine the sense of helplessness Brown must have endured. Though Brown never talked of the loss, Middleton supposed Street was the closest thing to a brother that Brown had ever known in these parts. The reverend was also aware of Brown's marital difficulties. Middleton had long figured that Brown's wandering eyes would result in trouble, but that problem seemed to be all ironed out. As they sat together under the stars, Middleton couldn't help but think that Brown was at peace with himself.

"Middleton," Brown began, interrupting the reverend's reflections, "I've joined the Theosophical Society."

His companion nodded. "Can't say as I'm much surprised."

The damn thing just makes so much sense to me," said Brown. "Life isn't about material possessions, about getting one up on your neighbor."

"No argument from me on that," replied Middleton.

"I've been halfway around the world, and seen so many religions…Hinduism, Christianity, Buddhism, Indian spirituality. I can't see how it is that a person's salvation is a result of where they're born, or how they're raised," Brown continued. "We're all just men, thrown into this world, acting out a play against a great cosmic backdrop. The secret to understanding is in a personal relationship with nature, one that lets us know our own true selves. It's not to be found in some manmade religion."

"Christianity is hardly manmade, Brown," suggested Middleton, "but I don't need to remind you of that. As for those other religions, well, greater men then I have noted that God works in mysterious ways. It's His time and His plans that matter. Seems to me, though, that your path is a pretty lonely one. No matter how you cut it, we're all part of a greater community, and it's up to each one of us to improve that community for the benefit of all."

"I left that community some time ago," Brown replied softly. "What it offers appeals to the worst in us, not the best."

"But how do we know what the best in us is, if we don't confront the worst?" asked the reverend.

"Rest assured, Middleton," replied Brown, "I know exactly what the worst in me is. I've faced it, struggled with it. It's discarded now, left in the dust-pile of ignorant and youthful—and even not so youthful—experience. My journey is, for the most part, a lonely one. It can't be undertaken bowing to the dictates of others."

"We do each have our own paths to follow," agreed Middleton.

"The best I can to is help those who, like me, are seekers," Brown concluded.

With that, the men rolled out their blankets and drifted off to sleep, one comforted by faith in God's designing hand, the other content to be a bit player in the great cosmic theatre.

WATERTON LAKES NATIONAL PARK
1899-1916

KOOTENAI BROWN EMERGED from the 1890s with a new perspective on life. He had confronted crises and demons. As he entered his 60s, he had weathered the former and wrestled the latter to the ground. He finally knew who he was and, more importantly, he was comfortable with that knowledge. Sure, the fiery temper could still resurface, but these years saw a much more patient and easygoing man. His greatest challenge proved to be a long-time interest of his: conservation. Brown threw himself into the expanded protection of Kootenay Lakes with a fervor typically known only by those on a religious mission. It turns out that he was truly a man blessed. He lived to see the fruits of his efforts.

By the time they turn 60, most folks start thinking about a slower pace to life, about gradually winding things down. A leisurely retirement, however, was not in the cards for a homesteader, especially one who had no children to rely upon. Brown found himself in just such a situation. His children were long gone, although he maintained a

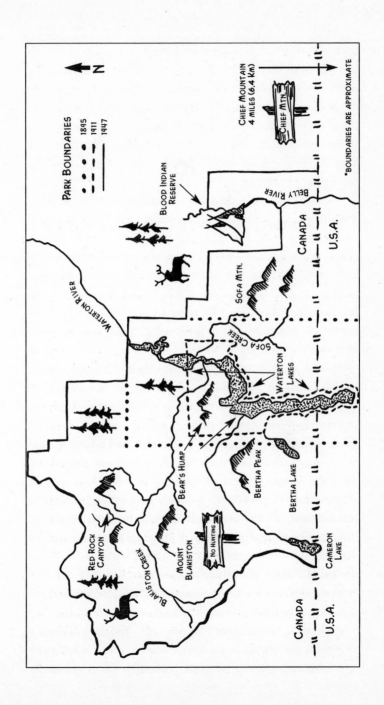

long-distance relationship with his son, Leo. As the 19th
century gave way to the 20th, Brown found it increasingly
difficult to maintain a decent standard of living pursuing
his traditional interests. With more and more people settling in the area, Brown noticed that animals were harder
to find and the lakes were getting fished out. And the settlers also brought inflation. The prices of most goods were
becoming exorbitant.

So, unlike those folks who envision relaxation in their
golden years, Brown discovered that he needed a new
source of income. He found that source with the federal
civil service. For the final 15 years of his life, Brown served
in a variety of capacities, all of them to do with protecting,
promoting and sharing the place he called home. However,
one shouldn't be misled by Brown's need for money. This
line of work was a labor of love as much as it was a pursuit
of pecuniary interests.

Brown was able to find employment in the conservation
field because of political developments in the Kootenay
Lakes region. In 1895, the federal Department of the
Interior had established the Kootenay Forest Reserve, a
small, undeveloped reserve of a township and a half that did
not include the Kootenay Lakes themselves. Stretching
from the northern end of Lower Kootenay Lake to the
international boundary, it was used mostly for picnicking
and camping by the residents of nearby Fort Macleod,
Pincher Creek and Cardston. The protection enjoyed by
the reserve was minimal—timber and oil resources could be
exploited under permit. Ultimately, it was the rapid development of the oil industry that resulted in greater protection for the region.

Although people knew oil reserves existed in the early
1890s, the boom that accompanied those initial discoveries
was short lived. It wasn't until businesses like the Rocky

Mountain Development Company and the Western Oil & Coal Company turned their efforts to the Kootenay Lakes region around the turn of the century that the oilmen's presence became disruptive. By 1905, conservation-minded individuals pointed out that entrepreneurs had bought up more than half the land set aside in the reserve. Those interested in preserving the natural beauty of the region began a campaign to get the federal government to address their concerns. The lobby group included Kootenai Brown and ranchers such as F.W. Godsal, as well as more influential folks such as John Herron, the local Member of Parliament.

Their initial efforts met with limited success. Federal officials tended to be more interested in the positive financial gains of resource development than they were with conservation. Even so, it was recommended that a forest reserve be created which would include the Kootenay Lakes. This recommendation was acted upon and in 1906 the area around the lakes, 15 kilometers long and 10 kilometers wide, became known as the Kootenay Lakes Forest Reserve. Administration of the reserve was placed under the authority of the superintendent of forestry in Ottawa.

New federal government legislation was passed in 1911 that drastically changed the situation in the reserve. The *Dominion Forest Reserves and Dominion Parks Act* stated that lands situated within forest reserves were to become Dominion parks. The administration of the parks was also placed under a commissioner of the Dominion Parks Service, a body of the Department of the Interior. One immediate effect was the creation of the Waterton Lakes National Park and an adjacent and enlarged Rocky Mountains Forest Reserve. The park was smaller than the old Kootenay Lakes Forest Reserve. At 35 square kilometers,

Oil City, located along Cameron Creek about eight kilometers (five miles) from the Waterton townsite, is the site of western Canada's first producing oil well, known also as Original Discovery #1. In 1878, A.P. Patrick, a Dominion surveyor, drilled a primitive well, but it was not until 1901 when Patrick, John Leeson and a local rancher, John Lineham, formed the Rocky Mountain Development Company that serious drilling began. They struck oil at 300 meters (985 feet) in August of 1901, and people were swept up in hopes of a local boom. Unfortunately, the well fell far short of expectations. Its production proved erratic, and it was finally closed just five years later, in 1906, after producing just 201 barrels. A cairn in the shape of an oil rig marks this historic site.

not much more than the mountain slopes on the west side of the lakes were protected.

About this time, government officials began to develop the region so that the park would be a more attractive tourist destination. A local townsite was surveyed in 1910, and in 1911 accommodations for visitors were constructed. Visitor services also began to proliferate; boats and trail horses were soon available. Roads were improved and automobiles became common, a sight that always remained slightly out of place for Brown. With the increase in the park's popularity, and increased pressure from local residents, the park's boundaries were substantially extended in 1914 to include some 1100 square kilometers. The decades that followed saw the park reduced in size, but its main features included Waterton Lakes valley, the southern reaches of the Belly River valley, the southeastern range of the Canadian Rocky Mountains west to the British Columbia border and the shared international boundary with the U.S. Glacier National Park.

Kootenai Brown could claim, without exaggeration, to have been not only a driving force behind the reserve's creation but also the most significant voice in its later expansion. It's hardly misleading to suggest that his life up to the age of 60 was but a precursor to the monumental impact he was to have in his final 15 years. Brown's conservationist passion was fuelled by a desire to protect the region for the enjoyment of everyone. No longer was he propelled by selfish motives, whether his own or those of individuals anxious to exploit the region's resources for their own financial gain. Brown's efforts, and they were colossal for a man of any age, were directed at ensuring that others could derive the same pleasure from Kootenay Lakes that he did. And those pleasures were considerable indeed.

ฦ

On October 10, 1900 (Brown's 61st birthday) the federal Department of Marine and Fisheries named
Kootenai Brown the fisheries officer for the region. The
creation of the position was an indication from the government that some proactive form of conservation
around Kootenay Lakes was necessary. Brown took up his
post at the beginning of 1901. For the most part, at least
initially, the job kept him in the outdoors that he enjoyed
so much. During the fishing season, he patrolled the lakes
and ensured that no one was pursuing illegal activities.
But a stream of paperwork increasingly came to dominate
his activities as a civil servant. Brown made reports on
water and weather conditions and on fish catches, and
he issued reams of licenses. It was a position he retained
until 1912.

Though it helped, the pay wasn't great. Initially he
received $50 a year, a sum increased in later years to $2 a
day while the fishing was active. To make ends meet, he
continued to offer his outdoor skills for hire as he had done
in past years. He advertised his guiding services to anyone
interested in exploring the region, be they tourists, hunters,
fishermen or prospectors. He also continued with his old
pursuits of hunting, fishing and breaking horses for the
Mounties. Still, money was tight. Some time earlier he had
unloaded the half-section of land he had received as partial
payment for his stint as a Rocky Mountain Ranger, and
taken out a homestead on a quarter-section with a more
desirable location and better hay for his horses. He sold this
quarter-section to the Western Oil & Coal Company for
$2000. It was a good time to sell because the oil boom had
inflated prices. It was an odd choice of buyer, though—at
about the same time, Brown had begun to publicly decry

the detrimental effects of the oil industry on the region. However, money was money, and potential buyers weren't exactly lining up at his door.

In 1908 the government of Alberta named Brown "Game Guardian" of the region. Though the position gave him another credential, both the work and the remuneration were limited. He sold game licenses to hunters, receiving a small commission on each one. However, his responsibilities increased dramatically a couple of years later when he was appointed a forestry ranger.

Brown had long been friends with John Herron, the local Member of Parliament. Their shared interest was the desire to preserve the natural surroundings of the Kootenay Lakes region. As Herron pressured the federal government to take a more active presence in local conservation issues, he regularly sought out Brown's advice. Their correspondence indicates that Brown was especially concerned with the increased number of visitors who were often careless in their recreational activities. More than once he had found campfires left burning by those long departed for home. Herron informed the Forestry Department that Brown was willing to take on the responsibility of patrolling the region, and further recommended that he was ideally suited for such a position. In those days of government patronage, the recommendation was quickly acted upon.

Brown's work up to this point as a civil servant had been a summer holiday compared to the activity involved in this new position. The physical demands were almost unimaginable. He rode nearly 400 kilometers a month. In winter, he stabled the horse and donned snowshoes. He traveled to Pincher Creek for supplies. When park employees agitated for an eight-hour day, Brown wrote to his superiors that ten hours better reflected a fair day's work.

For all intents and purposes, Kootenai Brown became the park's public relations man. He publicized the area, writing letters to organizations and newspapers. He dealt with complaints, and as much as possible he made certain that conditions were suitable for tourists. He oversaw commercial developments and made efforts to ensure that they did not unduly infringe upon the region's natural beauty. He initiated and was closely involved with park improvements, ranging from surveying and leasing Waterton townsite to cutting a horse trail in the southern reaches of the park. The trail connected with a pre-existing wagon trail in Glacier National Park, south of the international boundary, an important step in linking the two parks. Brown had long been of the opinion that the two parks should enjoy an uninterrupted continuity.

Brown's paperwork increased exponentially. He compiled records and wrote annual reports to the commissioner of national parks. While in his early 70s, Brown learned how to use a typewriter! After all, he was a man who was, for the most part, flexible in outlook. For all this effort he was paid $85 a year. He thought this inadequate and continually pressed for a raise that was never forthcoming.

Brown continued to pressure the Dominion government for changes in policy and development that would enhance the usability of the park. He wrote of his displeasure over the $1 camping fee, noting it was both unpopular and onerous. He drew comparisons to the United States' efforts to develop and conserve Glacier National Park and found the Canadian efforts wanting. Another plan suggested building a bridge across the Waterton River. In spring, when the mountain runoff swelled the river, the waters were difficult and dangerous to ford, as Brown and some companions discovered when they nearly drowned attempting the feat.

Brown was a colorful character, his scruffy moustache and slouchy hat becoming a trademark. He had a reputation in southern Alberta as a font of local information. He became a warden and forestry and fishing officer, working hard to protect the region he loved so much. His life encompassed the transition from the plains way of life to settlement, from hunting buffalo on horseback to riding around in a car. Kootenai Brown was a legendary figure of the West, his enduring bequest being the area he lobbied so strongly to protect, Waterton Lakes National Park, now a jewel in the crown of the Rocky Mountain parks system.

Without a bridge, much of the forest reserve on the western side was isolated and inaccessible to tourists.

Brown was also a persistent agitator for expanding the park's boundaries; he was particularly concerned that such a small area (prior to the park's expansion in 1914) would not offer adequate protection for wildlife. Wildlife preservation was an important issue to Brown because he was confident that the region would draw increasing numbers of hunters as knowledge of the local bounty became more widespread. For that reason, the news, in 1911, that the park was to be decreased in size was devastating for him. At the same time, the Kootenay Forest Reserve changed names to become Waterton Lakes National Park, and Brown was none too pleased. At best, Charles Waterton, the namesake, had only a superficial connection with the region. An English aristocrat and naturalist, Waterton had never even visited Alberta. Thomas Blakiston, a naturalist who accompanied Captain John Palliser on his explorations of Rupert's Land in the 1850s, had christened the lakes Waterton. Brown considered the change in names to be an example of modern officialdom at its worst—and an egregious slight to the region's true history. Brown figured that the Natives would soon enough be all killed off, or so mixed up with the white folks that they might as well be dead. The names they left behind would be the settlers' only memory of them.

The conclusion of Brown's career as a civil servant was bittersweet because it came just as his hopes for the park were finally realized. The news that the size of the park was to be dramatically increased was accompanied by the arrival from Ottawa of P.C.B. Hervey, the chief superintendent of national parks. As Hervey surveyed the new park, he concluded that it demanded a superintendent. Casting his eyes upon Kootenai Brown, he saw a man in the twilight of his years, one unable to properly administer the vast region.

Perhaps he was correct. Brown was headed into his mid-70s, although the regimen he followed would have exhausted a man half his age. When the first superintendent for the newly christened Waterton Lakes National Park was announced, it was Robert Cooper.

No longer motivated by money or position, Brown continued to offer his advice and to carry out his patrols as a ranger. But the long rides of yesteryear were increasingly adventures of memory.

ॐ

While the demands of a park ranger were rigorous, a considerably mellowed Brown found time to enjoy himself. Often his passions and work nicely dovetailed. He rode and enjoyed the outdoors as he had for the greater part of his life. He told stories to those thirsting for the adventurous times of the old West. To many who visited the park, the man in the Stetson who rode so tall and easily on his horse and who could tell a tale about just about any event from the region's history *was* the old West. Kootenai Brown was linked with the days of romance long gone.

Though Kootenai and Isabella Brown were the only homesteaders in the region well into the first decade of the 20th century, it could no longer be said that the Browns lived a lonely or solitary existence. Although some of Brown's best pals were long gone—Jack Street had died in an avalanche; Fred Kanouse had moved to British Columbia; and John Herron was often away on politics— there were others who still called regularly on the Brown homestead. Joe Cosley, a United States forest ranger, was a frequent visitor. Cosley was a renowned mountain trapper whose knowledge of the Waterton Lakes region was said by

some to be unmatched by any man, including Brown.
Frenchy Riviere, and Marie Rose Smith and her husband
William Gladstone, were among a handful of Métis who
were regular guests. And hands from nearby ranches or constables on patrol from their foothills detachment could
always be counted upon to punctuate any frontier monotony. Isabella's relatives also showed up from time to time.

The trips to town petered off over the years. Finally, in
1913, Brown bought a small frame house in Fort Macleod
and moved permanently from his homestead. Being in
town meant that Kootenai and Isabella had more time to
visit with others. On one such occasion, they were in
nearby Pincher Creek and had dropped in on their friends
the Staffords. After a couple of hours of chewing the fat,
Brown claimed that he needed a little fresh air. Fact was, he
wanted to see the children. Brown had discovered that with
age he had a new appreciation for childhood. And the children certainly loved him.

Brown found the kids playing outdoors. "So, your
friends here are from Medicine Hat?" he asked as he seated
himself on the stump of what had once been a massive tree.
"I don't suppose you boys know how Medicine Hat came
to be called Medicine Hat, do you?"

"No, sir," came the chorus of replies.

"Why don't you boys gather around and we'll have us a
little history lesson."

The boys sat down around Brown's feet. The old man
took off his Stetson, pulled his moustache down straight
and began.

"The medicine in Medicine Hat's got nothing to do
with the remedies that you get from the doctor. No, sir. It's
got to do with the Indians. If something is lucky, they say it
has good medicine. But if something doesn't turn out right,
well, they say it's bad medicine."

Brown and his wife Isabella. Kootenai's home was the first post office in the area and was owned by the Parks branch. By this time, Brown had become the area's spokesperson, continually pressuring the government for changes in policy and development for the park as well as pressing for an expansion of its boundaries to protect the natural wildlife. He was displeased with the $1 camping fee and found Canadian efforts to develop and conserve the park lacking when compared with those of the United States and Montana's Glacier National Park. He was far from pleased when he learned that the Kootenay Forest Reserve was to be renamed the Waterton Lakes National Park. Charles Waterton had never even been to Alberta, but the name had been chosen by Thomas Blakiston, a naturalist who had been a part of the Palliser Expedition.

"One time my pa won $10 on a horse race," one of the boys interjected. "Right after that, he went and got an old horseshoe from that horse. Does that horseshoe have good medicine?"

Brown laughed. "That'd be just the kind of thing I'm talking about. Now, there was a time when no white folks lived in Medicine Hat. In those days, people then just called the place Seven Persons' Creek. The only folks you were likely to see there were Indians. Back then, there were two great and powerful Indian nations, the Blackfoot and the Cree. They didn't like each other much. Matter of fact, they'd fight each other whenever they got the chance."

"Sounds like Ma and Pa," said one of the boys.

"Maybe so," chuckled Brown. "One day, the Blackfoot and the Cree stumbled upon each other at Seven Persons' Creek. The Blackfoot chief was wearing a handsome feather hat. That was his good medicine. Story goes that one time he was being chased by half a dozen Cree. To escape, he hid under a big bush and the Cree rode right past him. He figured that the hat was good medicine, and after that he never rode against the Cree unless he was wearing it."

Brown glanced at each boy and continued, "So anyway, back at Seven Persons' Creek, the Cree and the Blackfoot stood almost face to face, separated only by the water. The Blackfoot outnumbered their enemy, so they figured they'd have an easy victory. Suddenly a wind came up and the Blackfoot chief's hat was blown off his head and swept into the creek."

Brown tossed his hat across the clearing for effect.

"The chief watched as his hat sank under the surface," Brown continued. "This was real bad medicine. Rather than fight a battle he was sure they'd lose, the chief took his braves and ran for the mountains. The Cree considered this a great victory. Since that time, the place has been known as Medicine Hat."

There wasn't a child who encountered Brown who wasn't entranced by the magic of his stories. The relationship was one long remembered; when the YMCA established their boys' camp in the area in the 1930s, they called it Camp Inuspi—to remember the name the Natives had given to Brown because of his long hair.

Brown also devoted much of his time to writing and reading. He kept up regular correspondence with his son, Leo, and his old traveling companion from way back, Arthur Vowell. He also took to keeping a diary. Daily events were carefully recorded, and occasionally an original poem might appear.

Brown's intellectual interests in his later years were eclectic. While he closely followed the predictions of the French clairvoyant Madame de Thebes, he rarely discussed political or national matters. He subscribed to a variety of magazines and papers, ranging from *The Strand* to *San Francisco Weekly* to the local papers. He also frequently bought books and pamphlets from the Theosophical Society.

Brown's passion for philosophy was particularly evident. Classical writers and theosophical thinkers were often quoted in his writings, and sometimes Brown would include his reflections on their thoughts. His personal library, full of books on such matters, provided plenty of intellectual fodder. He wasn't stingy with either his thoughts or his books, sharing them with whoever demonstrated an interest. Isabella was not among this number, however. Her simple tastes were a reality that Brown had learned to accept, though there can be little doubt that it was one facet of his life that he must not have found fulfilling.

His great love over these years, however, remained the park. He returned there often and especially enjoyed the visitors and the opportunity to spin a yarn And the opportunities were plentiful. On one of his patrols, Brown rode east, close to the park's boundary. His eyes caught sight of a slight wisp of smoke rising straight up and he made his way toward it. He found three men seated around a fire, enjoying the shade provided by Chief Mountain.

"Howdy," Brown called as he drew near to the party. "I'd say that you boys have the right idea on day like today. Nice and cool here." He untied his handkerchief from around his neck, and mopped off his wet face. "Name's Brown. I'm the local ranger."

"I'm Peckham. This here's Kales and over there is Smitty. Take a load off your horse and join us for a cuppa," invited Peckham.

"Good of you to offer," Brown said. "You folks from around here?"

"Nope," replied Kales. "We're eastern boys, looking to make a go of it."

"You have a good eye. A man can't do much better than plant roots in this part. You're aware, though, that right around here is the Kootenay Reserve? Protected by the Dominion government?"

"That so?" replied Smitty. "Well, fact is we weren't planning on settling right here. This mountain was just such a sight that we'd figured on takin' a closer look at it."

"I can sure understand that," said Brown, nodding his head. "It's called Chief Mountain."

"Odd name," said Smitty.

"It's got a story," Brown chuckled. "Like so much else around here, the story is linked to the Indians. Care to hear it?"

All readily agreed. Brown adjusted himself on the log he was using as a seat and began the tale of Chief Mountain.

"This story comes by way of a ranger down at Glacier National Park, just south of the border. He claims he was told the story by a Blackfoot half-breed. The story takes place, oh, a good 80 years ago. Back in those days, the Blackfoot ruled this land pretty near all the way to Hudson Bay. Times weren't always good, though, and in the 1830s they suffered through a terrible drought. It was so bad that even the buffalo didn't come north. The Blackfoot were literally starving." Brown chewed on his moustache.

"There was one patch of grass, in the Two Medicine Valley just over yonder," said Brown, pointing his hand in its direction. "Desperate and out of options, some of the old men of the tribe decided to go to Two Medicine and pray to the Great Spirit. They asked the Great Spirit what they could do to end the famine. The Great Spirit heard their prayers. He told them to send seven of their elders to Chief Mountain. There they would find the Wind God, who would assist them."

Brown watched the smoke rise above the fire and said, "The Blackfoot followed the instructions of the Great Spirit. When they arrived at Chief Mountain, they found the Wind God, just like the Great Spirit said they would. The Wind God was a majestic and fearsome presence. He stood atop the mountain, his extended wings quivering as they covered all the nearby valleys and peaks. He seemed to look in all directions at once."

He paused for effect, then continued, "Well, the elders took one look at this and decided that they weren't going to go to the Wind God and pray. They were terrified!"

"No kiddin'!" Peckham interjected with a laugh.

"Yup," Brown chuckled. "So instead, the Blackfoot worshipped from afar. They soon returned to their people without a solution to their problem. The medicine men huddled together to consider this new problem. They finally decided to send 14 of their bravest warriors to the Wind God." He stopped and cleared his throat.

"When the 14 warriors arrived at Chief Mountain, they also found themselves full of fear. But they were courageous. They climbed the mountain until they could at last touch the Wind God's thick and rich skins. As the god looked down, the braves began to pray. Ever so slowly, the Wind God began to flap his wings. As he did, great clouds—first white and then dark—began to gather over the land. The clouds opened and rain fell as if from a pump."

Brown continued, "The Wind God pointed one of his wings to the east. 'Return,' he commanded, 'and you shall find the buffalo.' The braves quickly descended from the mountain and hurried back to their people. Upon their return, they discovered the buffalo already there. The famine was over."

There was a long pause as the three easterners considered Brown's story.

"You don't believe in that nonsense, do you?" asked Kales at last.

"Well, it doesn't rightly matter if I do believe it," Brown replied, "although the famine and its end are historical facts. And certainly the Indians believed it. The only thing I can say for certain is that I've seen *enough* in this world to know that I haven't seen *everything* in this world."

The group again fell silent. Finally Brown stood up.

"I've got to be getting back. You fellows enjoy yourself—but not too much," he said, nodding toward the nearby whisky jug. With a wink, Brown mounted his horse and vanished on the westward trail.

EPILOGUE

HIS STORIES—including the story of Kootenai Brown himself—did survive, but time finally caught up with Brown in
1916. In his last years as a ranger, the rides became shorter and
more of a challenge. Since being replaced as park warden,
Brown had been increasingly ill. He turned to whisky for its
medicinal effects, but it brought none of the pleasure of the
gallons swallowed long ago. He'd curse Isabella for watering
the hooch down, but she'd rightfully protest her innocence.
The whisky wasn't losing its kick; Brown was losing *his*.

In May, after falling ill and rallying, Brown wrote to his
son, Leo, asking him to come and take care of Isabella. He
suggested that she would be a good help to him. She certainly had been to Brown. Then Brown wrote his will, leaving everything to his wife. The requests in his testament
were few and simple. He wanted Leo, Vowell and the
Theosophical Society of America to be notified of his
death. He also indicated that he did not want any clergy
present in an official capacity at his burial.

Perhaps Brown was able to make one last ride to the
beloved park that he had done so much to create. Perhaps
he even got to see Sheep Mountain, his favorite hunting
spot in the region, one last time. Perhaps he was only able
to dream of such things before he died on July 18.

Brown was interred before a small but emotional group of mourners. A local Protestant minister led the ceremony. He was buried next to his first wife, Olivia, near the site of his first homestead on the shores of Lower Waterton Lake. Isabella would join them there in 1935. Whether she ever saw Brown in another form is unknown, but one can be sure that she never stopped looking.

NOTE ON SOURCES

A number of sources have figured prominently in the writing of this book. William Rodney's academic study, *Kootenai Brown: His Life and Times, 1839–1916* (Sidney, BC: Gray's Publishing Ltd., 1969), is an invaluable source of information. A short, popular account may be found in a book by S.H. Middleton (writing as Chief Mountain), *Kootenai Brown* (Lethbridge, AB: 1954). "I Remember," a regular column written by W. McD. Tait, appeared in the *Farm and Ranch Review* (1919–20). Tait was an associate of Brown in his later years and spent much time interviewing him. Marie Rose Smith reminisced about her friendship with Brown in a number of pieces collectively called "Eighty Years on the Prairies," found in *Canadian Cattlemen* (1949). For those interested in the Rocky Mountain Rangers, Hugh Dempsey published an article on the troop, under the same name, in the *Alberta Historical Review* (Volume 4, Number 2, 1957).

As much as possible, the words spoken by Brown in this book are his own, and the accounts are fictionalized as little as possible.